Social Issues
in Literature

Teen Issues in S.E. Hinton's *The Outsiders*

Other Books in the Social Issues in Literature Series:

Social Issues in Literature

Teen Issues in S.E. Hinton's *The Outsiders*

David E. Nelson, Book Editor

GREENHAVEN PRESS
A part of Gale, Cengage Learning

GALE
CENGAGE Learning

Detroit • New York • San Francisco • New Haven, Conn • Waterville, Maine • London

Elizabeth Des Chenes, *Director, Publishing Solutions*

© 2012 Greenhaven Press, a part of Gale, Cengage Learning

Gale and Greenhaven Press are registered trademarks used herein under license.

For more information, contact:
Greenhaven Press
27500 Drake Rd.
Farmington Hills, MI 48331-3535
Or you can visit our Internet site at gale.cengage.com

For product information and technology assistance, contact us at

Gale Customer Support, 1-800-877-4253
For permission to use material from this text or product, submit all requests online at
www.cengage.com/permissions

Further permissions questions can be emailed to permissionrequest@cengage.com

Articles in Greenhaven Press anthologies are often edited for length to meet page requirements. In addition, original titles of these works are changed to clearly present the main thesis and to explicitly indicate the author's opinion. Every effort is made to ensure that Greenhaven Press accurately reflects the original intent of the authors. Every effort has been made to trace the owners of copyrighted material.

Cover image © freelanceartist/Shutterstock.com.

LIBRARY OF CONGRESS CATALOGING-IN-PUBLICATION DATA

Teen issues in S.E. Hinton's The outsiders / David E. Nelson, book editor.
    p. cm. -- (Social issues in literature)
  Includes bibliographical references and index.
  ISBN 978-0-7377-5809-2 (hardcover) -- ISBN 978-0-7377-5810-8 (pbk.)
  1. Hinton, S. E. Outsiders. 2. Teenagers in literature. I. Nelson, David E.
  PS3558.I5480989 2012
  813'.54--dc23

                                                                    2012006898

Printed in the United States of America
  2 3 4 5 6   16 15 14 13 12

FD223

Contents

Hinton's writing for adults, although often lean and well crafted, cannot match her young adult work, including *The Outsiders*. Her young adult novels draw their energy from their honest depiction of the taboos that define teen life.

The Outsiders offers an interesting and nuanced analysis of class and gender. While wealth and social class seem to liberate the Socs, Hinton also seems to argue that class condemns them to rigid gender roles. Meanwhile, by virtue of their tough image, greasers are able to engage in what would otherwise be unacceptably feminine behavior.

Chapter 3: Contemporary Perspectives on Teen Issues

In July 2008 Nebraska enacted a "safe-haven" law that, due to its wording, made it possible for a parent to legally abandon his or her children at any Nebraska hospital. During the few months this law was in effect, thirty-five children (many of them "troubled teens" from out of state) were dumped at Nebraska hospitals, their parents driven by financial crisis or other desperate circumstances.

Introduction

In 1965, when fifteen-year-old Susan Eloise Hinton began pecking out her tale of teen drinking, violence, and class inequality, the word "teenager" was only twenty-three years old. The whole concept of "teenagers"—as a group distinct from children or adults—had only gained traction about sixty years before. With that in mind, it is clearly appropriate that it was a teenager who found a whole new way of talking about being a teenager.

Our modern idea of adolescence as a vital intermediate developmental period of "storm and stress" is generally credited to pioneering American psychologist G. Stanley Hall, who announced his "discovery" in the 1904 book *Adolescence: Its Psychology and Its Relations to Anthropology, Sociology, Sex, Crime, Religion and Education.* Prior to Hall the consensus had been that there were babies (who often did not survive infancy), children (who needed to be minded and educated), and adults (who worked, married, and raised their own families). The transition between the latter two categories might be gradual, with children beginning to take up adult responsibilities largely between the ages of ten and seventeen, but there was no notion that this was a separate stage of life with any lasting significance.

As is ever the case, the "discovery" of this new stage of American life brought with it new, specialized products. Among the first products specifically marketed to adolescents were novels and fiction magazines. The birth of "young adult" literature coincides with Hall's second major work, *Aspects of Child Life and Education,* which captured the growing belief among educators that children and adolescents would be best served by their own distinct literature, something more substantial than the simple and didactic McGuffey Readers used in schoolrooms. This period saw the launch of such venerable series as the Hardy Boys, Boxcar Children, and Nancy Drew.

It is important to note, however, that this early young adult literature was fundamentally different from "real" novels. In the adult literary world a novelist generally writes as an expression of introspection, using words to "look inward" and sort out his or her own feelings and experiences. Often penned by teachers or former teachers, these relatively new children's and young adult books were not an outgrowth of any legitimate literary movement but were instead the result of theories rooted in child psychology and educational reform. These books were thus fundamentally outward looking: They were written by adults not for themselves, but for groups that they felt were inherently different from, and lesser than, themselves. Early young adult literature was meant to teach moral lessons, bolster reading skills, and sell books. The few pieces of legitimate literature that did sneak into the young adult canon by the early 1960s (such as Harper Lee's *To Kill a Mockingbird* or J.D. Salinger's *The Catcher in the Rye*) are notable because they were written by adults *for an adult audience* and only later caught on with adolescents, hinting at an underlying—and underfed—teen appetite for real literature.

By the time Hinton began her debut novel in 1965, young adult novels were primarily written by middle-aged adults and were almost painfully out of touch with the interests and concerns of teens. The young adult books of 1965 were either adventure tales (such as the Hardy Boys or Nancy Drew) or teen romances of the "Janey goes to the prom" variety. They were light fare, inoffensive, and nakedly commercial: Often ghostwritten, books in these series were churned out quickly to be sold in soda shops and drugstores and to rake in teen dollars. In booming post–World War II America, teens increasingly had both disposable income (from part-time jobs or weekly allowances doled out by parents in the expanding middle class) and free time (as fewer teens had to pitch in around family farms and businesses in order for the family to survive).

Although Hinton, like many of her peers, enjoyed this same level of freedom previously unknown to fifteen-year-old American girls, by 1965 she was as badly in need of a place to sort out her feelings and experiences as J.D. Salinger or Harper Lee had been. Hinton's father was dying from a brain tumor. As her mother spent increasing hours at the hospital, Hinton spent more and more time in her room, writing. "Susie was very close to her father," Hinton's mother told Yvonne Litchfield of the *Tulsa Daily World* in 1967, on the occasion of the publication of *The Outsiders*, "and I noticed that the sicker [her father] became the harder she worked." This is, perhaps, what made all the difference: For the first time someone was writing for teens not because she wanted to teach them a valuable lesson, and not because she wanted to bolster literacy, and not because she wanted to get rich, but because she needed a break from the very real pains of the world. The place that she took shelter was in an abandoned church where Ponyboy and Johnny smoked cigarettes, read *Gone with the Wind*, and hid from a callous world that had set them up to fail.

This is how Hinton, entirely accidentally, re-formed the world of young adult literature. By writing an honest novel that sought to do nothing more (or less) than give her a place to sort out her own feelings, Hinton ushered in an era of stark "YA realism" that, once it is acknowledged as a peer to "real" novels, will be recognized as one of the most vibrant, alarming, and influential movements in twentieth-century American literature. The selections that follow explore Hinton's life, the varied critical responses to *The Outsiders*, and the current state of many teen issues addressed in Hinton's landmark debut.

Chronology

1950

Susan Eloise Hinton is born on July 22 in Tulsa, Oklahoma (although her birth year is disputed, and may be as early as 1948).

1965

Hinton, a high school sophomore, begins writing *The Outsiders* during her father's illness.

1967

Hinton graduates from Will Rogers High School in Tulsa, contracts with Viking Press to publish *The Outsiders*, and begins studying education at the University of Tulsa. *The Outsiders* is published in the fall.

1970

Hinton graduates from the University of Tulsa and marries David Inhofe, a software engineer.

1971

Hinton publishes *That Was Then, This Is Now* and receives an American Library Association Best Books for Young Adults award.

1975

Rumble Fish is published and receives the American Library Association Best Books for Young Adults award for that year and is named among *School Library Journal*'s Best Books of the Year. *The Outsiders* is named one of the Best Young Adult Books by the American Library Association.

1979

Hinton publishes *Tex*, earns the American Library Association Best Books for Young Adults award and the *School Library Journal*'s Best Book of the Year award.

1981

Tex is nominated for the American Book Awards.

1982

The first screen adaptation of one of Hinton's novels, *Tex*, is released by Disney Films.

1983

Films of *The Outsiders* (March 1983) and *Rumble Fish* (October 1983) are released, both directed by Francis Ford Coppola with Hinton cowriting the screenplays. Hinton gives birth to her son, Nicolas David Inhofe.

1985

That Was Then, This Is Now is released as a film. *The Outsiders* is adapted for television.

1988

Taming the Star Runner is published and wins the American Library Association Best Books for Young Adults award. Hinton earns the Young Adult Library Services Association's first Margaret Edwards Award for her body of work and its evocative depiction of the experiences and emotions of young people.

1995

Hinton publishes her first children's books: *Big David, Little David* (a picture book) and *The Puppy Sister* (a chapter book). *The Puppy Sister* wins a Parent's Choice Silver Honor.

1997

Hinton is recognized with the Oklahoma Center for the Book's Arrell Gibson Lifetime Achievement Award.

1998

Hinton is inducted into the Oklahoma Writers Hall of Fame at Oklahoma State University.

2004

Hinton publishes her first adult novel, *Hawkes Harbor.*

2006

Hinton publishes *Some of Tim's Stories,* her first collection of short fiction.

Background on
S.E. Hinton

The Life and Works of S.E. Hinton

J. Sydney Jones

J. Sydney Jones has written more than a dozen books. His non-fiction has included travel guides and histories, while his fiction ranges from a young adult novel set in the American West to a series of mysteries set in turn-of-the-century Vienna.

*In the following essay, Jones gives a brief overview of S.E. Hinton's life and writing. Since Hinton has spoken little about her personal life—even her birth date is disputed—the author primarily focuses on Hinton's novels and children's books as the benchmarks in her life. According to Jones, Hinton's first four young adult novels—*The Outsiders; That Was Then, This Is Now; Rumble Fish, *and* Tex—*can be seen as a single four-part progression, tracking Hinton's development as an author and a person.*

Ponyboy. Greasers vs. Socs. For millions of fans around the world, these few words will instantly call up the world of *The Outsiders*, S. E. Hinton's classic novel about teen gangs and the troubled process of fitting in. Since publication of this first novel in 1967, "the world of young adult writing and publishing [has] never [been] the same," according to Jay Daly in the critical study, *Presenting S. E. Hinton*. Daly went on to note that "*The Outsiders* has become the most successful, and the most emulated, young adult book of all time." Ironically, this quiet revolution in book writing and publishing was wrought by a seventeen-year-old girl, who by all rights should have been one of the intended readers of the novel, not its author.

Gale Group, *Something About the Author*, vol. 115. Farmington Hills, MI: The Gale Group, 2000. Copyright © 2000 by Cengage Learning. All rights reserved. Reproduced by permission.

A Major Shift in Young Adult Lit

Susan Eloise Hinton was a high school sophomore at Tulsa's Will Rogers High School when she began her novel. At the time she had not the slightest dream in the world that her manuscript would be published, let alone that it would sell millions of copies worldwide, spawn a motion picture, and start a trend in publishing toward gritty realism for younger readers. At the time, young Susie was simply working out private concerns. Firstly, she was reacting to divisions apparent in her own high school, and secondly, she was filling a void in subject matter that she herself wanted to read. At the time when Hinton began writing, young adult titles were mostly pure as corn and sweetly innocent; tales in which the major problem was which dress to wear to the prom or whether such-and-such a boy would be the date. "Into this sterile chiffon-and-orchids environment then came *The Outsiders*," observed Daly. "Nobody worries about the prom in *The Outsiders*; they're more concerned with just staying alive till June."

If Hinton turned the world of publishing upside down with her youthful title, its publication did the same for her life. As word of mouth slowly made the book a classic (it [as of 2000] has eight million copies in print), Hinton was attempting to develop a normal life, studying education at the University of Tulsa, marrying, and having a family. Writing block settled in and it was four years before her second title, *That Was Then, This Is Now*, came out, another edgy story of teen angst. Two further books were published in four-year intervals: *Rumble Fish* in 1975, and *Tex* in 1979. Then nearly a decade passed before publication of her fifth YA title, *Taming the Star Runner*. Since that time, Hinton has published two titles for younger readers. Small in output, Hinton has nonetheless made a major impact on children's literature, a fact confirmed by the 1988 presentation to her of the first annual Margaret A. Edwards Award for career achievement. Her books [as of 2000] have over ten million copies in print; four of her five YA titles have been filmed; and Hinton still receives bushels of mail from enthusiastic fans for all her books, but especially for *The Outsiders*, now over three decades old, but with a message that continues to speak across the generations.

An Active Tomboy Withdraws

Hinton was born in 1948, in Tulsa, Oklahoma, but little more is known about her early years, as Hinton herself is a very private person. Indeed, confusion reigns around aspects of her life, such as her year of birth as well as her inspiration for beginning to write. What is known is that she grew up a voluntary tomboy in love with horses. That passion has not diminished over the years, and Hinton is still an avid horsewoman. She was able to use her horse lore in the novel *Taming the Star Runner*. Hinton's tomboy status also brought her closer to male friends than female. She identified more with active males than with the passive role females of the day were encouraged to project.

A self-confessed outsider as a youngster, Hinton did not belong to any one clique in school, but was friends with a wide variety of types. Along with horses Hinton also developed an early love of reading. "I started reading about the same time everyone else did," Hinton wrote in *Fourth Book of Junior Authors*, "and began to write a short time later. The major influence on my writing has been my reading. I read everything, including Comet [cleanser] cans and coffee labels." Her first writing efforts dealt with horses, and her stories were generally told from a boy's point of view. By the time she reached high school, she was ready to tackle a larger subject, namely the rivalry between two groups in the school, the "greasers" and the affluent "socs" (short for "socials").

In the wake of school shootings across the nation during the 1990s, all Americans have become more sensitive to the outsider groups at schools, to the cruel pecking orders established in the microcosm of schools. In Hinton's day, peer pressure was no less severe and oppressive. "I felt the greasers were getting knocked when they didn't deserve it," Hinton told an interviewer for *Seventeen* shortly after publication of her novel. "The custom, for instance, of driving by a shabby boy and screaming 'Greaser!' at him always made me boil. But it was the cold-blooded beating of a friend of mine that gave me the idea of writing a book."

Hinton began the writing in her sophomore year, during the time her father, Grady P. Hinton, was diagnosed with a brain tumor. As Daly put it, "It is not something she talks about, but one gets the impression that his hospitalization, and the inevitable, unavoidable conclusion that his illness promised, were factors in her withdrawing into herself." While her mother spent more and more time at the hospital, Hinton spent more time in her room or at the dining room table working on her novel. "Susie was very close to her father," Hinton's mother told Yvonne Litchfield of the *Tulsa Daily World*, "and I noticed that the sicker he became the harder she worked." Hinton's father died in her junior year, about the time she completed her book.

The Outsiders Gathers a Following

Hinton worked through four drafts of her story before she was happy with it, but still she gave no thought to publication until the mother of one of her school friends—a professional children's writer—took a look at the manuscript. This reader immediately saw commercial possibilities for the book and urged Hinton to get in touch with her own New York agent. The Oklahoma teenager did just that, and the rest is publishing history.

Hinton's novel was, as Hinton myth has it, accepted for publication the night of her high school graduation, and it appeared in bookstores the spring of her freshman year at college at the University of Tulsa. As the book was written from the male perspective, Hinton's publisher, Viking, prompted her to adapt the more genderless author name of S. E. Hinton. Such a publication was an enormous gamble for a prestigious New York house, but Hinton's book was no overnight success. Slowly and by word of mouth sales grew and continued growing. Letters started arriving at the Hinton household from teenagers all over the country confessing that they never imagined somebody else felt like they did, that they were solaced by the fact that others felt like outsiders just as they did. It was soon apparent that Hinton had touched a raw nerve in American culture. . . .

A Sentimental but Effective Novel

Critical reception of this publishing phenomenon was mostly laudatory; those with reservations mostly found the book erred on the side of over-sentimentality and clichéd writing. "Can sincerity overcome cliches?" asked Thomas Fleming in the *New York Times Book Review*. Fleming answered his own question mostly in the positing: "In this book by a now 17-year-old author, it almost does the trick. By almost any standard, Miss Hinton's performance is impressive." Fleming's view was reflected by other reviewers, both then and now. Writing in [the literary journal] *Horn Book*, Jane Manthorne called Hinton's work a "remarkable novel . . . a moving, credible view of the outsiders from inside." Lillian N. Gerhardt, reviewing the novel in *School Library Journal*, drew attention to the rare fact in juvenile novels of "confronting the class hostilities which have intensified since the Depression." Gerhardt noted that "Ponyboy . . . tells how it looks and feels from the wrong side of the tracks." Reviewing the book in *Atlantic Monthly*, Nat Hentoff lamented the sometimes "factitious" plot, but declared that Hinton, "with an astute ear and a lively sense of the restless rhythms of the young, also explores the tenacious loyalties on both sides of the class divide." Hentoff concluded that the book was so popular among the young "because it stimulates their own feelings and questionings about class and differing life-styles." An English reviewer for the *Times Literary Supplement* cut to the chase when noting that it was largely irrelevant whether adult reviewers found the novel dull, contrived, over-sentimentalized, too violent, or just plain implausible. "Young readers will waive literary discrimination about a book of this kind and adopt Ponyboy as a kind of folk hero for both his exploits and his dialogue," the reviewer concluded.

In the event, this critic was dead on. Once word of mouth was established regarding the youth and gender of the writer of *The Outsiders*, sales continued to grow and grow. It was apparent that Hinton and Viking had struck an entirely untapped readership: young kids aching for their stories to be told from their point of view with their voice. Little matter that Hinton's supposed stark realism was really "mythic" as the critic Michael Malone pointed out in an extended piece on the author in [the] *Nation*. "Far from strikingly realistic in literary form," Malone remarked, "[Hinton's] novels are romances, mythologizing the tragic beauty of violent youth. . . ." Malone and others have rightly pointed out that the vast majority of teenagers personally experience nothing close to the violence of Hinton's characters, nor do they suffer the vacuum of parental supervision of her Peter Pan–like cast of orphans and near orphans who must look after themselves or watch out that alcoholic, abusive parents do not do them harm.

Never mind, either, the fact of Hinton's sometimes "mawkish and ornate" prose, according to Malone who noted that Ponyboy "fling[s] adjectives and archaic phrases ('Hence his name,' 'Heaven forbid') around like [author] Barbara Cartland." Ponyboy, through whose eyes the action is viewed, describes characters with an elevated language that is often inappropriate to his spoken thought; he is also prone to quoting [poet Robert] Frost. But never mind any of this; Ponyboy and his cast of friends and foes alike are romantic representations, not the viscerally realistic depictions they are usually labeled.

S.E. Hinton and Matt Dillon on the set of the 1982 film adaptation of Hinton's novel Tex, *a collaboration that began a lasting friendship between the author and actor.* © Michael Ochs Archives/Stringer/Moviepix/Getty Images.

Gene Lyons, writing in *Newsweek*, got it right: "The appeal of Hinton's novels is obvious. . . . The narrator-hero of each is a tough-tender 14- to 16-year-old loner making his perilous way through a violent, caste-ridden world almost depopulated of grownups. 'It's a kid's fantasy not to have adults around,' says Hinton. While recklessness generally gets punished, her books are never moralistic—all manner of parental rules are broken with impunity."

Writer's Block

Royalties from *The Outsiders* helped to finance Hinton's education at the University of Tulsa where she studied education and where she met her husband, David Inhofe. But for several years Hinton suffered from writer's block so severe that, as she told Carol Wallace in the [*New York*] *Daily News*, she "couldn't even write a letter." In an interview with Linda Plemons in the *University of Tulsa Annual*, Hinton confessed that "I couldn't write. I taught myself to type in the sixth grade, and I couldn't even type or use my typewriter to write a letter. Things were pretty bad because I also went to college and started reading good writers and I thought, 'Oh, no.' I read *The Outsiders* again when I was 20, and I thought it was the worst piece of trash I'd ever seen. I magnified all its faults."

Finally, after she decided that teaching was not for her, and with encouragement from Inhofe, Hinton sat down to write a second novel. Setting herself the goal of two pages a day, Hinton had, after a few months, a rough draft of the novel *That Was Then, This Is Now*. Once again Hinton sets her action in the same Tulsa-like surroundings, and focuses on an orphan, Mark, who has lived with the narrator, Bryon, and Bryon's mother since his own parents killed each other in a fight. It is now over a year since the ending of *The Outsiders*, and the old gang and social rivalries are not as clear-cut as they once were. The days of hippies are at hand; drugs are part of the teen landscape. One of the characters, M&M, is a proto-hippy whose LSD overdose tips the balances between Bryon and Mark. No angel himself, Bryon turns in his foster brother for supplying M&M with drugs. There is gang violence aplenty, teens on the prowl and on their own—Ponyboy Curtis even makes an appearance. Overall the book is more disciplined than Hinton's first title, but as Daly and other critics pointed out, "it lacks something." For Daly, it was the inspirational "spark" missing that kept it from breathing true life as had *The Outsiders*.

Other reviewers, however, found Hinton's second novel a moving and heartfelt cry from yet another teenager in pain. For Michael Cart, writing in the *New York Times Books Review*, Bryon's struggles with his future and with those he loves form the core of the book. "The phrase, 'if only' is perhaps the most bittersweet in the language," Cart noted, "and Miss Hinton uses it skillfully to underline her theme: growth can be a dangerous process." Though Cart had problems with Bryon's ultimate "life-denying self-pity," turning against his love and life, he concluded that Hinton created "a mature, disciplined novel, which excites a response in the reader. Whatever its faults, her book will be hard to forget." Reviewing the novel in *School Library Journal*, Brooke Anson remarked that the book was an "excellent, insightful mustering of the pressures on some teen-agers today, offering no slick solutions but not without hope, either." *Horn Book*'s Sheryl B. Andrews found that this "disturbing" and "sometimes ugly" book "will speak directly to a large number of teen-agers and does have a place in the understanding of today's cultural problems." Selected a Best Books for Young Adults in 1971, *That Was Then, This Is Now* confirmed Hinton as more than a one-book author.

Mixed Reviews for *Rumble Fish*

Another four years passed between publication of *That Was Then, This Is Now* and Hinton's third novel, *Rumble Fish*. Hinton's narrator, Rusty-James, is another classic sensitive outsider type, who begins his narrative with the blunt declaration: "I was hanging out at Benny's, playing pool, when I heard Biff Wilcox was looking to kill me." Rusty-James's older brother, Motorcycle Boy, something of a Dallas Winston clone, meets a violent death in the novel, echoes of Dallas's demise in *The Outsiders*. And like Hinton's other novels, *Rumble Fish* takes place in compressed time, focusing on incidents which change the life of the narrator forever. Dubbed Hinton's "most ambitious" novel by Geoff Fox and George Walsh writing in *St. James Guide to Children's Writers*, the novel deals with Rusty-James's attempts to make some meaning of life after the passing of the gang conflicts that made his brother such a hero. Now, however, Motorcycle Boy is disenchanted, without hope, and virtually commits suicide, gunned down breaking into a pet store. By the end of the novel Rusty-James is left on his own, having lost his brother, his reputation, and his girl, and is without direction. As Jane Abramson noted in *School Library Journal*, "it is Rusty-James, emotionally burnt out at 14, who is the ultimate victim." Abramson concluded that the "[s]tylistically superb" *Rumble Fish* "packs a punch that will leave readers of any age reeling." Some reviewers, such as Anita Silvey in *Horn Book*, found the novel unsatisfying and Hinton's further writing potential "unpromising."

Rumble Fish did have admirers both in the United States and abroad. A *Publishers Weekly* contributor declared that "Ms. Hinton is a brilliant novelist," and Margery Fisher, writing in England's *Growing Point*, commented that "once more is the American urban scene in a book as uncompromising in its view of life as it is disciplined." While others complained of too blatant symbolism in the form of Motorcycle Boy and the fighting fish that give the book its title, Fisher concluded that "Of the three striking books by this young author, *Rumble Fish* seems the most carefully structured and the most probing." Exploring themes from aloneness to biological necessity. *Rumble Fish* tackles large questions in a small package. As Daly concluded about this third novel, "In the end we respond to *Rumble Fish* in a much deeper way than we do to *That Was Then, This Is Now*. It's an emotional, almost a physical response, as opposed to the more rational, intellectual reaction that the other book prompted." Daly went on to note that despite its defects in too-obvious symbolism, it "works as a novel. . . . And there is a name usually given to this kind of success. It is called art."

Hinton herself noted that she had been reading a lot about color symbolism and mythology when writing *Rumble Fish*, and that such concerns crept into the writing of the novel, especially in the character of Motorcycle Boy, the alienated, colorblind gang member looking for meaning. Hinton begins with character, as she has often noted in interviews, but in *Production Notes* for *Rumble Fish*, the screenplay of which she co-wrote with Francis Ford Coppola, she remarked that the novel "was a hard book to write because Rusty-James is a simple person, yet the Motorcycle Boy is the most complex character I've ever created. And Rusty-James sees him one way, which is not right, and I had to make that clear. . . . It's about over-identifying with something which you can never understand, which is what Rusty-James is doing. The Motorcycle Boy can't identify with anything."

Hinton's Most Accompished Novel

The standard four years passed again before publication of Hinton's fourth title, *Tex*, which was, according to Daly, "Hinton's most successful effort" to date. Once again the reader is on familiar ground with near-orphan protagonists, and troubled youths. With *Tex*, however, Hinton opts for a more sensitive and perhaps less troubled narrator than before. Tex McCormick is, as Hinton noted in Delacorte Press's notes from the author, "perhaps the most childlike character I've ever done, but the one who makes the biggest strides toward maturity. I have to admit he's a favorite child." Of course this was several years before the birth of Hinton's own son, Nick.

Another fourteen-year-old lacking parental supervision, Tex has his older brother Mason to look after him while their father is on the rodeo circuit. A story of relationships, Hinton's fourth title focuses on the two teenagers at a time when Mason has had to sell off the family horses to pay bills, as no money has come from their father. This includes Tex's own horse, Negrito. Straining already strained relations between the brothers, this loss of a favored animal sets the plot in motion. Tex tries to run off and find the animal. Neither his friend Johnny nor Johnny's sister Jamie (the romantic attachment) is able to talk Tex out of it, but Mason drags him home in the pickup. Johnny and Tex are forever getting in trouble and things get rougher between Mason and Tex by the time the two brothers are kidnapped by a hitchhiker (Mark from *That Was Then, This Is Now*, who has busted out of jail). Tex's presence of mind saves them, but gets Mark, the hitch-hiker, killed by the police. Notoriety at this brings the father home, but disappointment follows when he fails to track down Negrito as he promised. More trouble—in company with Johnny and then with a former friend of Mason's who now deals drugs—lands Tex in the hospital with a bullet wound. He learns that his real father was another rodeo rider, gets a visit from Johnny and Jamie, and once recovered and recon-ciled with Mason, convinces his older brother that he should go on to college as he's wanted to. Tex tells him he's lined up a job working with horses and can take care of himself.

"Hinton's style has matured since she exploded onto the YA scene in 1967," noted Marilyn Kaye in a *School Library Journal* review of *Tex*. Kaye felt that Hinton's "raw energy . . . has not been tamed—its been cultivated." The outcome, said Kaye, "is a fine, solidly, constructed, and well-paced story." *Growing Point*'s Fisher once again had high praise for Hinton, concluding that "In this new book Susan Hinton has achieved that illusion of reality which any fiction writer aspires to and which few ever completely achieve."

Notable Film Adaptations

Hinton's re-created reality was strong enough to lure Holly-wood. Disney productions bought the rights to *Tex*, filming a faithful adaptation of the novel with young Matt Dillon in the lead role, and introducing actors Meg Tilly and Emilio Es-tevez. Shot in Tulsa, the movie production used Hinton as an advisor, introducing Dillon to her own horse, Toyota, which played the role of Negrito, and teaching the young actor how to ride. It was the beginning of a long and continuing friend-ship between Hinton and Dillon, who played in three of the four adaptations of her novels. The movie also started a trend of introducing young actors on their way up in her movies.

Next to get a film treatment was *The Outsiders*, though not from Disney this time but from Francis Ford Coppola of *Godfather* fame. Somewhat operatic in its effect, the movie cast Dillon as Dallas Winston, and also starred such future luminaries as Patrick Swayze, Rob Lowe, Tom Cruise, and Estevez. Coppola also filmed *Rumble Fish*, shooting it in black and white to resonate with Motorcycle Boy's color blindness. Once again Dillon starred, with Micky Rourke as Motorcycle Boy. Dennis Hopper, Tom Waits, and Nicolas Cage rounded out the cast. The script was co-written by Hinton and Coppola. In both the Coppola adaptations, Hinton played bit parts as well as worked closely as an advisor during production. However, with the fourth movie adaptation [of *That Was Then, This Is Now*], from a screenplay by Estevez and starring him, Hinton remained on the sidelines. Thus, within a few short years—from 1982 to 1985—all of Hinton's novels were turned into movies and her popularity was at an all-time high, with movie sales driving up book sales. Hinton had the added plus in that her experience with movies was a very positive one. "I really have had a wonderful time and made some very good friends," Hinton told Dave Smith of the *Los Angeles Times* regarding her work with Coppola. "Like a lot of authors, I'd heard the horror stories about how they buy the property and then want the author to disappear and not meddle around worrying about what they're doing to the book. But that didn't happen at all. They invited me in right from the start, and I helped with the screenplays." . . .

An Enduring Legacy

Hinton has focused on family in recent years, and on her hobby of horseback riding. She is reportedly at work on another YA novel, though there are no indications whether or not she will return to her outsider themes. "I don't think I have a masterpiece in me," Hinton once told Smith in the *Los Angeles Times*, "but I do know I'm writing well in the area I choose to write in. I understand kids and I really like them. And I have a very good memory. I remember exactly what it was like to be a teenager that nobody listened to or paid attention to or wanted around." In the three-plus decades since Hinton herself was a teenager, things have changed very little. The street kids, the gangs, the cliques at school that drive kids to extremes: these are all still at play, and Hinton's novels speak to teens as strongly now as they did at the time of their publication.

S.E. Hinton on *The Outsiders* and Young Adult Literature of the 1960s

S.E. Hinton, as told to Lisa Ehrichs

Lisa Ehrichs interviewed S.E. Hinton for the November 1981 issue of Seventeen *magazine. Founded in 1944, Seventeen is among the fifty most widely circulated magazines in the United States, serving an audience of girls aged twelve to nineteen.*

The following interview was published just a year before the first film adaptation of a Hinton novel—Tex—arrived in theaters. Although these film adaptations (especially that of The Outsiders, *released in 1983) would transform Hinton into a household name, she was already a remarkably popular—and young—novelist at the time. In this interview, Hinton discusses why she wrote* The Outsiders *and her other gritty young adult novels and offers advice to young writers.*

*T*he Outsiders, a tough yet sensitive novel about a gang of teenagers from the wrong side of the tracks, was a major success for author S.E. Hinton when it came out in 1967. Its publication marked the beginning of a new category of young-adult literature: novels that looked beyond the narrow world of the high school prom. But the most remarkable thing about *The Outsiders* is that its author, Susan Eloise Hinton, was only seventeen when the book was published.

Ms. Hinton followed *The Outsiders* with three other novels, *That Was Then, This Is Now; Rumblefish;* and *Tex*. In 1970, she graduated from the University of Tulsa, in Oklahoma, and continues to live in Tulsa with her husband. Below, Ms. Hinton talks about her early success as a novelist and gives advice to today's young writers.

Taking Time to Define Characters

Lisa Ehrichs: How did you first become interested in writing?

S.E. Hinton: I started in grade school—it was just something I enjoyed doing. I was the type of girl who loved horses and cowboys, so I wrote about them. I read a lot and had fun making up my own stories. Though it was the first one published, *The Outsiders* was actually my third book. I found that for me, novels were easier to write than poems or short stories.

Why is writing a novel easier?

A novel gives you time to define characters, and characters are my strong point. I think about them until I know everything there is to know about each of them.

What made you write The Outsiders?

I'd wanted to read books that showed teen-agers outside the life of "Mary Jane went to the prom." When I couldn't find any, I decided to write one myself. I created a world with no adult authority figures, where kids lived by their own rules.

How long did it take you to write it?

The Outsiders took me a year and a half. During that time, I did four complete drafts. The first draft was forty pages; then I just kept rewriting and adding details.

Pitfalls of Being a Young Writer

How did you get it published?

It was amazingly easy. A friend gave me the name of an agent [from Curtis Brown, Ltd., in New York] who read it and liked it. He thought he could sell it and did—to Viking, the second publisher we tried!

What kinds of problems did you face as a young writer?

The publisher thought that my being a teen-age writer was a good gimmick, and my close friends thought it was neat. But people I didn't know too well started treating me as though I were stuck-up. I had always been a smart-alecky kid, but after the book was published, I knew I had to change or else people would think success was going to my head. So I became quiet—but people saw that as being stuck-up, too!

Why are your main characters, such as Ponyboy in The Outsiders *and Rusty-James in* Rumblefish *, always male?*

I started writing before the women's movement was in full swing, and at the time, people wouldn't have believed that girls would do the things that I was writing about. I also felt more comfortable with the male point of view—I had grown up around boys. But my female characters *will* be getting stronger.

Advice to Young Writers

In what ways do your characters reflect aspects of your own personality?

The characters have to be part of yourself, you have to understand them. By the time they go through your head and work their way down on paper, they reflect some aspect of you. Ponyboy Curtis [the protagonist of *The Outsiders*] probably comes closest to me—he's absent-minded and quiet and daydreams a lot.

Why do you think you've been so successful as a writer?

I think it's because I remember how it felt to be a kid. It's not the happiest time, but if you hang on, it gets better.

Any tips for young writers today?

Read. Read everything you can get your hands on. I read a lot when I was younger, and I still do—it's almost an obsession!

Hinton on Her Work and Its Adaptation to Film

S.E. Hinton and Anne Commire

S.E. Hinton is the award-winning author of a number of young adult novels that have been adapted for film. Anne Commire edited a number of interviews of Hinton for the series Something About the Author.

In the following selection, largely composed of statements made by Hinton over the course of a dozen interviews, the author discusses her experiences working in Hollywood on the film adaptations of three of her young adult novels: The Outsiders, Rumble Fish, *and* Tex. *Hinton closely collaborated with directors and screenwriters on all three films, as well as working with actors during shooting. Despite her quiet upbringing in Tulsa—and herself being very shy—Hinton had an overwhelmingly positive experience and found herself a good fit for Hollywood, a community largely composed of social outsiders.*

Hinton continues to speak to teens. All four of her [young adult] books have been made into major Hollywood feature films; *Tex*, the first movie, released in 1982, was produced by Walt Disney. "At first I said, 'No, thank you, I'm not interested in doing a Disney movie.' I thought they'd really sugar it up, take out all the sex, drugs and violence and leave nothing but a story of a boy and his horse. Then Tom Wilhite, vice president at Disney, landed on my doorstep and convinced me that they wanted to broaden their audience and do a hard PG movie. I liked Tom Wilhite and agreed to sell on the condition that my horse got to play the lead horse. Those two deals happened within a week of each other."

Filming *Tex*

The shooting was done in Tulsa, and Hinton was involved in the casting, scriptwriting, and directing of her own work as a collaborator of director Tim Hunter. "Once I sold the books I expected to be asked to drop off the face of the earth. But that didn't happen. I know that I had extremely rare experiences for a writer. Usually the director does not say, 'Boys, these are important lines, so you've got to know them word for word. . . . '"

"I was just stunned that I liked all these movie people. I thought they'd all be money-grubbing, sex-crazed dope addicts, but they're not money-grubbing at all."

"But, on the other hand, I'm well aware that the writer is usually not the most respected member of the crew."

Working with Francis Ford Coppola

During the same period, a group of high school students from Lone Star, California sent a petition to Francis Coppola nominating him to make a movie of their favorite book, *The Outsiders*. Coppola's producer, Fred Roos recalled: "The jacket was so tacky. It looked like the book was privately printed by some religious organization. I carried it around with me for weeks, but I didn't open it. One day I found myself on an airplane, and I was tired of carrying it around. I said to myself that I'd give it ten pages. I ended up reading it cover to cover and I agreed with the kids. I thought it was a movie."

Roos highly recommended the project to Coppola who eventually contacted Hinton: "When I met Susie, it was confirmed to me that she was not just a young people's novelist, but a real American novelist. For me the primary thing about her books is that the characters come across as very real. Her dialogue is memorable, and her prose is striking. Often a paragraph of her descriptive prose sums up something essential and stays with you. . . ."

Hinton, who had turned down previous offers for the movie rights to *The Outsiders*, accepted Coppola's offer after being impressed by his screen adaptation of *Black Stallion*. As with *Tex*, she was on the set as a creative consultant. "When Francis visited me in Tulsa, he showed me how he was writing the screenplay. He had literally taken the book apart, outlining in red the sections with action and the passages of introspection in blue.

"Working with that guy is so funny. He can go forever and thinks that everyone else can, too."

"Halfway through 'The Outsiders,' Francis looked up at me one day and said, 'Susie, we get along great. Have you written anything else I can film?' I told him about *Rumble Fish*, and he read the book and loved it. He said, 'I know what we can do. On our Sundays off, let's write a screenplay, and then as soon as we can wrap *The Outsiders*, we'll take a two-week break and start filming *Rumble Fish*. I said, 'Sure, Francis, we're working sixteen hours a day, and you want to spend Sundays writing another screenplay?' But that's what we did."

". . . We were in his office for about twelve hours writing before I finally said, 'I can't go any further, I'm beat.' And he said, 'No, no, no! We'll put some more tapes on the machine. Here's another glass of wine. Stay, stay.'

"He put a tape of the Police on the machine and after a while he looked up and said, 'I really like that drummer. Get me that drummer!' And the next thing I knew Stewart Copeland was sitting in on the *Rumble Fish* rehearsals playing the drums so we could rehearse to his beat."

An Outsider Fits in Hollywood

"It's the first time I've ever felt at home in a group situation. I've never been a joiner. In Tulsa I have a reputation for being slightly eccentric. Even my close friends think I'm a little nutty. But with the movie people I was accepted instantly.

"Also, when you're making a movie, you feel like an outlaw. Traffic stops for you, and you don't keep the same hours that anybody else keeps. I like that outlaw feeling. And there's one other nice thing about the movies. There's always somebody else to blame. With a novel, you have to take all the blame yourself."

"I really have had a wonderful time and made some very good friends during the filming. Like a lot of authors, I'd heard the horror stories about how they buy the property and then want the author to disappear and not meddle around worrying about what they're doing to the book.

"But that didn't happen at all. They invited me in right from the start, and I helped with the screenplays. The scripts stick closely to the books, and so much of the dialogue is mine, so naturally I'm happy with them.

". . . I guess I thought I'd collect some really funny, cynical Hollywood stories. And that's where I got disillusioned. The movies are damn near as good as my books."

Working with a Young Matt Dillon

Rumble Fish and *The Outsiders* were both released in 1982 starring Matt Dillon, one of America's most successful teenage actors. "Matt identifies with Rusty-James [in *Rumble Fish*]. He told me a long time ago, when we were shooting *Tex*, that *Rumble Fish* was his favorite book. He said '[We] gotta get somebody to make a movie of it so I can play the part.' And I said that by that time, he might be too old; I asked him if he'd play the Motorycyle Boy. He said, '[Y]eah, and if I'm really old, like twenty-seven, I'll direct.'

"Matt is exactly the kind of kid I write about. Of course, he's a much more complex person than any of my characters, but he has facets of all of them. He has a sweet side, which was good for *Tex*, and that street-wise thing that got him through Dallas in *The Outsiders*, and a funny, charming cockiness that's perfect for Rusty-James.

"I love to see Matt walking around reading books. He had read all of mine before we ever met, and I feel I'm partly responsible for the fact that he likes to read now.

"I didn't know Mickey Rourke [Motorcycle Boy in *Rumble Fish*], but after Francis told me who he was, I remembered seeing *Body Heat* and thinking, when he came on the screen, 'I know that guy.' It was such a strong recognition factor. I wonder if it was a premonition."

Hinton Stays a Novelist

1985. Release of the movie *That Was Then, This Is Now*. While Hinton enjoyed working for the movie industry, her primary involvement as a writer continued. ". . . I still think of myself as a novelist, and with the next book I'm writing, I'm doing everything I can to make it unfilmable."

"I don't think I have a masterpiece in me, but I do know I'm writing well in the area I choose to write in. I understand kids and I really like them. And I have a very good memory. I remember exactly what it was like to be a teen-ager that nobody listened to or paid attention to or wanted around. I mean, it wasn't like that with my own family, but I knew a lot of kids like that and hung around with them. They were street kids, gang kids, sort of scrounging around, and somehow I always understood them. They were my type."

The Outsiders Continues to Touch Young Adults in the Twenty-First-Century

Connie Ogle

Connie Ogle is a widely read book and film critic. She has written for the Miami Herald *for more than twenty years. She also writes the* Herald's *books blog,* Between the Covers, *and has served as the* Herald's *book editor for a decade.*

In the following article, written in 2004, Ogle explores the ongoing popularity of S.E. Hinton's groundbreaking novel. She also talks with Hinton about her evolution as a writer, moving beyond young adult fiction, and what motivated Hinton to adopt a largely male perspective in her writing and to speak to specific audiences. Ogle discusses Hinton's non–young adult books, including children's books such as The Puppy Sister *and Hinton's 2004 vampire novel for adult readers,* Hawkes Harbor.

Maybe someday fans will stop asking about Ponyboy and his poor, doomed friend Johnny. Maybe they will no longer request that autographs include the haunting phrase "Stay gold," which, you may know, comes courtesy of [poet] Robert Frost.

But S.E. Hinton, author of *The Outsiders*, knows that time has not yet arrived. Still, while such popular fiction writers as Michael Chabon, Isabel Allende, Carl Hiaasen, Dave Barry and Elmore Leonard have been busy grinding out books for younger readers, the reclusive Hinton has shifted gears. She has just released her first adult novel, her first book in 15 years. But she knows the furor over *The Outsiders* isn't over.

The Outsiders Still Speaks to Teens

Written when Hinton was 16 and published in 1967, the novel about a group of kids growing up on the wrong side of the tracks has sold more than 10 million copies and was made into a movie by Francis Ford Coppola. These days, although you can cheat and buy the Cliffs Notes, young readers still connect with Hinton's compelling story of violence, loss, the need to belong and the bitter inequities of social structures.

"*The Outsiders* is the most distinctive young-adult novel of its tradition, the nonconformist prototype," says Sydna Wexler, section supervisor of youth services for Broward County (Fla.) Main Library. "All the middle-school students are reading it. Of all the novels I have spoken to students about, this is the one that's most asked for. We order it almost continuously. . . . Its universal truths and the message stand the test of time."

"I get all these letters, the same ones for 35 years: 'I didn't know anybody else felt like this,'" Hinton says from her home in Tulsa, Okla., where she grew up and now lives with her husband. "I go to fanfiction.com, and there are 900 stories about *The Outsiders*. They write prequels and sequels or take a minor character and make the story about them. I love that I have made a world kids want to inhabit. It's a good way for kids to learn to write.

"When I was a kid I wrote *Bonanza* fan fiction, all these stories about the Cartwrights. I didn't have anywhere to put it, but now kids do."

Taking a New Direction

The new *Hawkes Harbor* is quite a detour for Hinton, also known for the teen novels *That Was Then, This Is Now, Tex, Rumble Fish* and *Taming the Star Runner*. It does feature Hinton's trademark troubled young man who doesn't know quite where he fits in, but what haunts Jamie is a lot more tangible (and bloodsucking) than feelings of isolation.

At the 2009 Los Angeles Times Festival of Books, S.E. Hinton autographs a copy of her still popular first novel, The Outsiders, which was published in 1967, when she was seventeen years old. © Katy Winn/Corbis.

Still, "I don't think of it as a horror novel," Hinton says. "It's character-driven, like my other books. It's more the story of a man's life. I'm interested in the paranormal, but I don't believe in vampires. I'm more interested in using the idea as a character definition."

Hinton says she doesn't necessarily envision a particular audience but admits that the idea of an adult novel was appealing. With two young children's books under her belt—*The Puppy Sister* is about a little dog that believes she's a sibling, not a pet—"I got all the whimsy out of my system," she says. "Then I was living with a teenager [her son Nick, now in college]. It's hard work writing about them when you're living with one. But I did want to get back to writing for the fun of it."

In addition to spawning Grenville Hawkes, the haughty vampire who sincerely wishes to reform, *Hawkes Harbor* uncorked Hinton's sense of adventure, freeing her to imagine pirates, shark attacks and raunchy sex, none of which you find in most young-adult novels.

"It wasn't like I didn't know what I was doing when I wrote *The Outsiders*," Hinton says. "I'd been writing since grade school, because I loved to read. It was just the most fun thing I could think of to do besides ride horses." (She still rides, too.)

Hinton has always been drawn to characters with difficult childhoods, and Jamie is an orphan who works as a gunrunner. Ponyboy and his brothers were orphans, too. Hinton, whose father was dying of cancer while she was immersed in *The Outsiders*, writes almost exclusively from the male perspective.

The Freedom of the Male Narrator

"I had a tough childhood, not like my characters, but I understand it," she says. "I just like the way people who are uneducated in the ways of relationships kind of go out and get their own education.... When I grew up I was a tomboy most days. The sexes were so segregated. Most of my friends were guys, and I was an oddball.

"Nobody would have believed it if *The Outsiders* had been about girls. I didn't understand the female mind then. The story was set in the '60s, so no way could I write it from the viewpoint of young women. I enjoyed the freedom of the male narrator."

Hinton is working on a series of adult stories and mulling a supernatural western. She wonders if she can find inspiration in a back story set in Hawkes Harbor about Grenville's pre-vampire past. But you can be sure of this: She will not attempt a sequel to *The Outsiders*, no matter how hard you beg.

"I wrote it at the right time of life," she says. "The feelings you have at 16 you can't recapture. I'm not even certain if I will do another teen book. . . . I can't be a teenager again. *The Outsiders* was totally honest. That was the way I was feeling and observing. I was living that book."

Well, of course. As Ponyboy learned, nothing gold can stay.

Social Issues in Literature

CHAPTER 2

The Outsiders and Teen Issues

The Genius of *The Outsiders* Is in Its Honesty About Violence and Danger in Teens' Lives

Stephanie Zacharek

Stephanie Zacharek is a film, theater, book, and pop music reviewer best known for her decade-long stint writing film reviews for Salon. *She has also written for* Rolling Stone, Entertainment Weekly, Interview, *the* Village Voice, *and* New York *magazine.*

This essay is drawn from a 2007 review Zacharek wrote for S.E. Hinton's 2006 collection of short fiction, Some of Tim's Stories. *Zacharek argues that Hinton's writing for adults, although often lean and well crafted, cannot match her young adult work (something that Hinton herself has often highlighted). This is because Hinton's most notable works—which certainly include* The Outsiders—*draw their energy from Hinton's honesty about the complex taboos in teenage life, from smoking to violence, from sex to substance abuse. Hinton powerfully chooses to honestly depict these facts of teenage life rather than to condemn them.*

Before [the TV shows] *Buffy the Vampire Slayer* and *Veronica Mars*—but not before [the James Dean film] *Rebel Without a Cause* and [the 1960s girl group] the Shangri-Las—there was *The Outsiders* (1967), a novel by S.E. Hinton that cut to the heart of teenage anxiety and confusion as no other book had. Written in language whose rhythms felt true to the way kids talked, from the point of view of Ponyboy Curtis, a bright, idealistic 14-year-old who veers dangerously close to ending up on the wrong side of the law, *The Outsiders* had the vitality and the audacity of rock 'n' roll—partly because Hinton was a teenager herself when she wrote it.

Hinton's Collection

Inspired by the youth gang rivalries in her hometown, Tulsa, Okla., Hinton began writing *The Outsiders* when she was 15; she received the publishing contract on the day of her high school graduation. Even though *The Outsiders* represented the birth of a genre—previously, books for teenagers had focused mostly on dating issues or the woes of parent-child relationships—it was still, a year after its hardcover publication by Viking, just a paperback novel, the kind sold on squeaky drugstore racks. Just as it was set to go out of print, the paperback publisher, Dell, noticed an uptick in sales. Teachers had begun ordering multiples for their classrooms; they'd discovered that even teenagers who'd never finished a book in their lives would read *The Outsiders*.

In the years since, Hinton, who still lives in Oklahoma, has written eight books [as of 2007], some for young adults, others for children or for grown-ups. The latest, *Some of Tim's Stories*, is a compact set of vignettes about a young bartender named Mike and his conflicted relationship with his cousin, Terry: the two are closer than brothers, until a cruel twist drives them apart.

In a series of interviews that make up the second half of the book, Hinton explains that the "Tim" of the title is the writer of these stories. "Mike" is Tim's thinly disguised alter ego, a guy who can't stop punishing himself for the ways in which he might have failed his cousin. He loses the one woman he loves most, and he gets drunk more than he should. But he also enrolls, somewhat accidentally, in a fiction-writing class at his local community college, and writing becomes a way for him to cope with his fear and guilt.

Each of these stories is brief—several are just three or four pages—and Hinton trims her prose close to the bone. As Mike sits at his aunt's kitchen table, eating a sandwich she's prepared for him, Hinton, via Tim, takes one of his memories of growing up with Terry and carves it into a sharp, concise observation: "You two eat like horses for such skinny boys. They had heard that all their lives. Then they hit 20 and filled out, like someone had colored in an outline, and people said no wonder you two ate so much."

The Power of *The Outsiders*

But brevity can work against a writer, too, and even though these stories are admirably direct, they also feel truncated and at times incomplete. Suddenly, the truth hits: What's missing is the swaggering, dirty-dungaree dialogue of *The Outsiders* and the rambling yet weirdly concise interior monologues of Ponyboy, its confused but eminently likable narrator.

There's just no book like *The Outsiders*, and even Hinton seems to know it. The interviews with the author included in the collection—conducted by Teresa Miller, the founder and executive director of the Oklahoma Center for Poets and Writers and the editor of the University of Oklahoma's "Oklahoma Stories & Storytelling" series, of which this is the second volume—throw off more sparks than the stories themselves. Hinton (whose full name is Susan Eloise; her publishers advised her at the beginning to use her initials, to prevent readers from prejudging a woman author writing from a guy's point of view) says she believes Tim's stories are the best writing she's ever done. But she also seems to know she can't recapture the raw, youthful energy of her first book: "I don't compete with *The Outsiders*. It's there, I'm proud of it, but I'm through with it, like I am with Tim's stories."

An Honest Treatment of Complex Taboos

Could *The Outsiders*—or, for that matter, any of Hinton's other novels for young adults, including *That Was Then, This*

Is Now (1971) and *Tex* (1979)—even be written today? Among the numerous idiotic pronouncements people make about the past, whether we're talking 40, 60 or even hundreds of years ago, is "Those were more innocent times." Of course, any parent today will tell you that children are outgrowing childhood faster than ever, with toddlers requesting Bratz dolls and grade-schoolers taking weapons into class.

But part of what makes Hinton's books wonderful is the fearlessness with which she addressed all the things young people weren't, and still aren't, supposed to do: drag racing, fighting with knives (or guns) and, to name perhaps the most current taboo, smoking. Hinton's books, refreshingly nonjudgmental, weren't social tracts or cautionary tales designed to ward her readers off the things that might have killed them (although they might ultimately have had that beneficial effect). In *That Was Then, This Is Now*, the 16-year-old protagonist, Bryon, swings by the hospital room of a bandage-wrapped teenager who is in a great deal of pain after having been badly beaten. The kid begs Bryon for a smoke and Bryon obliges, holding a lit cigarette to the kid's lips.

The world of Hinton's young adult books isn't simpler or more innocent than the one we live in now. Yes, kids, smoking is bad, very bad! And even secondhand smoke can kill you. But does it hurt to be reminded that there once was a time, so very long ago, when sharing a cigarette could be an act of compassion, not corruption? Hinton may never top *The Outsiders*. But by telling it like it was, she left a record of the way things were—a record that can't be revised or erased, even after we've crushed that last Marlboro box and left it behind forever.

The Outsiders Gives an Unrealistic, Romanticized View of Teen Life

Michael Malone

Novelist Michael Malone is likely best known as a writer for the soap opera One Life to Live, *for which he garnered four Emmy nominations and one Emmy Award.*

In the following viewpoint Malone argues that, despite being heralded for its "gritty realism," The Outsiders *is a fairy-tale plot wrapped in purple prose. According to Malone, the novel's elevated language, stylized violence, and diehard platonic love clearly make* The Outsiders *a sort of mythic romance novel. Malone does not question the impact the novel has on readers, only the reasons for this impact: Rather than speaking to teens with its gritty depiction of real life, he believes,* The Outsiders *resonates with them because it speaks to the ideals they embrace and hope to embody.*

America at its saddest and dangerously silliest has the adolescent soul of a grade-B cowboy movie—violent and sentimental, morally and mentally simplistic. No doubt that's why a grade-B movie star [Ronald Reagan] still [as of 1986] sits tall in the saddle of the Oval Office, sometimes quoting [movie vigilante cop] Dirty Harry and sometimes teary poems. And no doubt that's why the four Young Adult novels of S.E. Hinton have sold millions of copies and have made their rough-tender way into successful Hollywood movies, usually starring Matt Dillon, one of teen-age America's heart-throbs. The novels—*The Outsiders; That Was Then, This is Now; Rumble Fish;* and *Tex* (Dell)—are touted on their covers as heroic tales of "the young and the restless," as "strikingly realistic portraits of modern kids trying to make it in a rough world." S.E. Hinton is the nom de plume of an Oklahoma woman, Susan Eloise Hinton, who publishes under her gender-anonymous initials because her books are first-person narrations of male teen-agers and, according to librarians, are read mostly by sixth- to eighth-grade boys. M.E. Kerr, another popular young adult novelist, uses the same strategy.

For Teens, by a Teen

Hinton was 17 when she wrote *The Outsiders*, and the characters, she says, were "loosely based" on people she knew. "When I was growing up, most of my close friends were boys," she remarked in an interview in *The New York Times*. "In those days girls were mainly concerned about getting their hair done and lining their eyes. It was such a passive society. Girls got their status from their boyfriends. They weren't interested in doing anything on their own." They certainly don't do anything on their own in Hinton's books—indeed they scarcely put in an appearance, although the male narrators frequently comment on how nice their hair looks. Nor are adults much in evidence. In this world the stories, like the streets, belong almost exclusively to tribes of adolescent males, to accounts of their tender camaraderie, reckless rebellion, macho warfare and often tragic fates.

It is difficult, if not horrifying, to think that the millions of 12-year-olds reading these "strikingly realistic portraits of modern kids" find any more in them than the most remote connections to their own lives, for Hinton's boys are usually impoverished, are often thugs and thieves, are variously abandoned by parents, brutalized by policemen, jailed, stabbed to death, shot to death, burned to death and so routinely beaten nearly to death that they think it's a drag to have to rush to the hospital for something as trivial as a fractured skull. When his chest is cut so deeply in a gang fight that he can see "white bone gleaming through," Rusty-James of *Rumble Fish* grits his teeth ("Ain't all that bad") while his brother douses whiskey on the wound ("He's been hurt worse than this!"). These are "lean hard"! "tough as nails"—or rather "tuff" as nails—"cool" 14-year-olds. Misery, lawlessness and violence are served up matter-of-factly to palates presumably so jaded by screen violence that it seems there are no squeamish stomachs left among the prepubescent. "The Dingo is a pretty rough hangout; there's always a fight going on there and once a girl got shot" (*The Outsiders*). "The last guy who was killed in the gangfights was a Packer. He had been fifteen" (*Rumble Fish*). Bryon, narrator of *That Was Then, This is Now*, comments blandly. "We fought with chains and we fought Socs and we fought other grease gangs. It was a normal childhood.... So that was how we lived, stealing stuff and selling stuff." Other boyish pastimes mentioned are drunken poker games, car theft, drag racing, pool hustling and "jumping hippies and blacks." The horrendous life of Bryon's former girlfriend is summed up in a paragraph and dismissed as nothing unusual: "Her husband didn't have a job, her brothers were both in jail, her old man was drunk all the time, and her father-in-law was always slapping her bottom.... They weren't so different from most of the families in our neighborhood."

Tragedy is parenthetical, introduced in a dependent clause: "Since Mom and Dad were killed in an auto wreck...." (*The Outsiders*). Even in *Tex*, the most recent, the least riddled with gang, romance and the best of the books, Tex (a pleasant fellow, given to believable classroom pranks and adolescent worries) is forced at gunpoint to drive an escaped killer to the state line. He rolls the truck into a ditch, enabling the pursuing police to blow the young convict away in a barrage of crossfire. Only a week or so later, Tex himself is critically shot in the stomach while accompanying a friend on a drug deal. Tex has only gone along for the ride because he's upset. He's upset because his brother has just blurted out that their Pop is not really Tex's father; his real father was a no-good rodeo cowboy with whom Mom had a one-night stand to spite Pop when he was in prison for bootlegging. . . .

Romantic Myth, Not Realism

What is clear from the recurrent themes of Hinton's novels, like the discovery of mysterious parentage, is that despite their modern, colloquial tone, they are fairy tale adventures (Luke Skywalker's father is really Darth Vader), and their rumbles as exotic as jousts in *Ivanhoe* or pirate wars in *Treasure Island*. What is curious is that grown-ups insist on the books' veracity. Hinton announces, "The real boy like Dallas Winston [the role Matt Dillon plays in *The Outsiders*] was shot and killed by the police for having stolen a car." Tim Hunter, director of the film *Tex*, says he was drawn to Hinton's work because of the way she weaves social problems "into the fabric of a realistic story."

In fact, the fabric is mythic. There are no verisimilar settings. Presumably the books take place near Tulsa, Oklahoma (the films do), but place names are never mentioned, and were it not for occasional references to rodeos, one would have little notion of the Western ambiance so evident in the movie versions. Characters live in "the neighborhood"; sometimes they go to "the city" or to "the country." The city is bacchanalian: "There were lots of people and noise and lights and you could feel energy coming off things, even buildings" (*Rumble Fish*). The country is pastoral: "The clouds were pink and meadowlarks were singing" (*The Outsiders*). Temporal location is equally vague. *The Outsiders*, published in 1967, might as easily have been written ten years earlier, in the fifties of its real progenitor, James Dean movies. True, some parenthetical hippies are up to some druggy no-good in *That Was Then, This Is Now* (1971), but the Motorcycle Boy in *Rumble Fish* (1975) might have ridden right off the screen of *The Wild One*. Far from strikingly realistic in literary form,

Ralph Macchio (left) as the vulnerable Johnny with Matt Dillon as Dallas and C. Thomas Howell as Ponyboy in the 1983 film version of S.E. Hinton's The Outsiders. © Sunset Boulevard/Corbis.

these novels are romances, mythologizing the tragic beauty of violent youth, as the flashy surrealism of Francis Ford Coppola's *Rumble Fish*, with its film noir symbolism and spooky soundtrack, all too reverently attests.

Lyric Prose, Not Realistic Dialogue

Moreover, while praised for its "lean Hemingway style" and natural dialogue, Hinton's prose can be as fervid, mawkish and ornate as any nineteenth-century romance, although this is less true in the later books, especially *Tex*. The heightened language of her young narrators intensifies the glamour and sentiment of their stories, but it will not strike readers as everyday school-locker lingo. Ponyboy, 14, and Bryon, 16, fling adjectives and archaic phrases ("Hence his name," "Heaven forbid") around like [novelist] Barbara Cartland. Bryon notes that his friend Mark's "strangely sinister innocence was gone." Ponyboy describes his brother, Sodapop, as having "a finely drawn, sensitive face that somehow manages to be reckless and thoughtful at the same time," as well as "lively, dancing, recklessly laughing eyes." Ponyboy is also given to quoting from memory long snatches of Robert Frost's "Nothing Gold Can Stay," and to using words like "merrily," "gallant" and "elf-ish." Of course, Bryon and Ponyboy point out to us that although they seem to spend all their time hanging out with the gang, they are both honor students: "I make good grades and have a high IQ." But even Rusty-James of *Rumble Fish*, stuck in "dumb classes" and, by his own admission, no student ("Math ain't never been my strong point"), waxes poetical: "I wouldn't have her to hold anymore, soft but strong in my arms." Sententious moralizing coats the pages: "That was what he wanted. For somebody to tell him 'No.' . . . If his old man had just belted him—just once, he might still be alive." "You start wondering why, and you get old." "We see the same sunset."

The lyricism, the lack of novelistic detail, the static iconography of Hinton's books keep the clutter of creation from interfering with the sources of their obviously persistent appeal—their rapid action (mostly violent) unfettered by the demands of a plot, their intense emotions (mostly heavy) and their clear-cut moral maps. Hinton's fictional universe is as black-and-white as an old cowboy film. *The Outsiders* is the ur-text. In it there are Socs (Socials) and there are greasers; unlike that of the warring Hatfields and McCoys, Montagues and Capulets, Jets and Sharks, this eternal enmity is neither familial nor racial, but financial. Socs are rich, greasers are poor; Socs are "the in crowd," greasers are "the outsiders." Socs always wear madras and English Leather and drive Mustangs or Corvairs. They always "jump greasers and wreck houses and throw beerblasts for kicks." That's pretty much all we get to know about Socs; they're just the enemy. A Soc girl, Cherry Valance, makes a brief appearance to point out to Ponyboy, "We have troubles you never even heard of," but those troubles are not explored; instead she schematizes neatly: "You greasers have a different set of values. You're more emotional. We're sophisticated—cool to the point of not feeling anything." Given this fundamental difference (and despite the fact that they see the same sunset), Cherry is obliged to warn Ponyboy: "If I see you in the hall . . . and don't say hi, well, it's not personal. . . . We couldn't let our parents see us with you all."

Our heroes, greasers, are also initially defined by their appearance and their style of antisocial behavior: "We steal things and drive old souped-up cars and hold up gas stations once in a while . . . just like we leave our shirt-tails out and wear leather jackets." But popular culture has taught us to interpret this style with sympathy, if not rabid infatuation. The narrators pay continual, indeed obsessive, attention to their own and their friends' appearance. We hear constantly about "strange golden eyes," "light-brown, almost-redhair hair," faces like "some Greek god come to earth." They are always asking and reassuring each other about their good looks, particularly the beauty of their hair. . . .

Absent Parents Replaced with Tribes

In Hinton's books, selfhood is subsumed in the tribal gang. "It was great, we were a bunch of people making up one big person" (*That Was Then, This Is Now*). "Why did the Socs hate us so much? We left them alone." "It wasn't fair for the Socs to have everything. We were as good as they were" (*The Qutsiders*). So magically does the gang incorporate its members that in the opening of *The Outsiders* it miraculously appears out of the night to save Ponyboy from the motiveless malignity of a carful of Socs: "All the noise I had heard was the gang coming to rescue me." "Somehow the gang sensed what had happened."

The gang is the family: "We're almost as close as brothers." And in contrast to "a snarling, distrustful, bickering pack like the Socs," greaser gangs are unfailingly loyal and free of rivalry. Maybe they have "too much energy, too much feeling, with no way to blow it off" except through marauding violence, but with one another they are as gentle as maidens on a Victorian valentine, innocently sleeping with their arms around each other, choking with tenderness for one another's pain. Johnny in *The Outsiders* is the most vulnerable, most pathetically hurt gang member (the Sal Mineo part in *Rebel Without a Cause*; for his film of *The Outsiders*, Coppola even found in Ralph Macchio an actor who looks just like Mineo). Ponyboy's solicitude for him is shared by even the toughest of the greasers. He is "a little dark puppy that has been kicked too many times and is lost in a crowd of strangers. . . . His father was always beating him up, and his mother ignored him. . . . If it hadn't been for the gang, Johnny would never have known what love and affection are." Like Mineo's Plato, Johnnycake is clearly pegged for fearful sacrifice. And sure enough—having accidentally stabbed a Soc to death and then redeemed himself by saving some children from a burning church—he dies from burns and a broken back after a series of heart-rending hospital-bed scenes. As might be expected in fiction for adolescents, the blood brother bond supersedes all other emotional commitments. *That Was Then, This Is Now* opens, "Mark and me went down to the bar"; and Bryon's love for Mark, like the love of [medieval heroes] Beowulf or Roland for their companions, runs like a lyric refrain through the novel. . . .

In *Rebel Without a Cause*, James Dean is trying to cope with a new society, with a new girl, with his parents, with adult authority. He copes in part by means of wry humor, a detachment that is missing in Hinton's books and in the films made from them. Rather than ask her characters to cope with adults, wryly or otherwise, Hinton either removes them or removes their authority. The Oedipal struggle is displaced to older siblings. Ponyboy's parents are dead; he lives with and is supported by his big brother, Darry, a football star who gave up college to keep the family together. Ponyboy fears and idolizes him. Tex's mother is dead (after a fight with his father, she walked off in the snow to go dancing, caught pneumonia and quickly succumbed), and his father forgets for months at a time to return home or to send money. Tex lives with and is supported by his older brother, Mace, a basketball star, whom he fears and admires. Rusty-James's mother ran away; his father, once a lawyer, is a hopeless drunk on welfare who wanders in and out of the house mumbling, "What strange lives you two lead," to Rusty-James and his idolized older brother, the Motorcycle Boy (about whom Hinton seems to feel much as Lady Caroline Lamb felt about Byron: "Mad, bad and dangerous to know"). Like Dallas Winston, the Motorcyle Boy is shot to death by the police, leaving the hero to inherit his romantic mantle—even to the extent of going color-blind. Bryon has no father but does have a mother, depicted as a model of saintly virtue. She behaves, however, with a remarkable lack of maternal responsibility or even curiosity. Not only do Bryon and Mark sometimes not "come home for weeks" without being reprimanded but their being beaten black and blue elicits little concern. Mom notices ten stitches in Mark's head: "How did that happen?" "And Mark answered, 'Fight,' and the subject was dropped. That was a good thing about Mom—she'd cry over a dog with a piece of glass in his paw but remained unhysterical when we came home clobbered. . . . Parents never know what all their kids do. . . . It's a law." The laws of Hinton's books are the laws of the cowboy movies, the laws of romance.

The Outsiders Demonstrates How Teens Can Transcend Socioeconomic Class Divisions

Michael Pearlman

Michael Pearlman taught at the University of Delaware in the Department of English, where he specialized in pedagogy and curriculum development.

In this article Pearlman notes that research has long established the degree to which socioeconomic status (SES) informs adolescent self-esteem. He suggests that authors of adolescent fiction are well aware of this and deploy socioeconomic status within their novels with two goals in mind. First, a character's socioeconomic status is used to help readers relate to and identify with the protagonist. Second, the characters' own views of socioeconomic status—and the way these views change over the course of the novel—is a fundamental element of the characters' development. Finally, authors use this combination of identification and demonstrated character development to teach readers how they can see beyond socioeconomic status in their own lives.

An important theme in adolescent literature is how the socioeconomic status (SES) of a character or characters acts to reinforce the author's moral purpose in writing the novel. Central to this idea is the presumption that SES plays an important role in the lives of adolescents, that the awareness of differing levels of SES strongly influences adolescents' self-perceptions as well as their perceptions of the external world. According to [M.] Rosenberg and [L.] Pearlin [in 1978], "Both

Michael Pearlman, "The Role of Socioeconomic Status in Adolescent Literature," *Adolescence*, vol. 30, 1995, pp. 223–232. Copyright © 1995 by Libra Publishers, Inc. All rights reserved. Reproduced by permission.

children and adults learn their worth, in part, by comparing themselves with others ... both children's and adult's self-attitudes are influenced to a large degree by the attitudes of others towards themselves." Authors of this literature are aware that adolescents are extremely aware that the SES of their literary characters greatly influences the perceptions readers form about these characters.

Four adolescent novels, *To Kill A Mockingbird* by Harper Lee, *The Catcher in The Rye* by J.D. Salinger, *The Pigman* by Paul Zindel, and *The Outsiders* by S.E. Hinton, reflect this influence. In each of these novels, the characters' relative SES plays an important role in the moral progression of the story and in the main characters' internal growth. Because of adolescents' concern with this factor, a character's SES dramatically affects the way he/she is perceived by the adolescent reader.

Relative SES and Self-Esteem

The findings of a number of studies on the relationship between adolescent SES and self-esteem level in the United States concur that in most cases, there is a strong positive and replicable correlation between these two variables. One study ... for the Pennsylvania Department of Education examined Pennsylvania public school students' levels of self-esteem. The self-esteem indicators were based on three categories: relationships with their teachers, relationships with peers, and their self-image in school. From 1981–84, 35,000–50,000 5th-, 8th-, and 11th-grade students were interviewed. The schools in the study were located in both high and low SES areas.

In this study, a "consistent pattern" emerged at all three grade levels. It was found that "self-esteem increased as SES level increased for students attending low SES as well as high SES schools. In fact, SES accounted for the highest percentage of variance in student levels of self-esteem."

Another study by [C.L.] Richman, [M.L.] Clark, and [K.P.] Brown [in 1985] corroborates these findings. "A significant main effect of SES was found for the Rosenberg [scale]:

"Low SES students had lower general self-esteem scores than the middle or high SES students."

[David H.] Demo and [Ritch C.] Savin-Williams (1983) argue that "the ascribed nature of social class among young adolescents makes it a weak determinent of their self-esteem, but that with increasing age socioeconomic position becomes more meaningful and thus consequential for self-esteem."

Scout and Jem, Holden, and Ponyboy

Authors of adolescent literature, aware of the strong SES consciousness among adolescents, incorporate characters in their novels with differing SES levels in order to create plots which have a more realistic appeal to their impressionable young readers. . . .

While wealth and acquisition are not primary to a character's sense of SES in *To Kill a Mockingbird*, the same is not true [for] *The Catcher in the Rye* where a clearly inverse relationship exists between Holden Caulfield's SES and his level of self-esteem. All indications in this novel point to the fact that Holden comes from an affluent family. His father is a corporate lawyer who can afford to buy his son a private education. Holden, in turn, squanders money throughout the course of the novel, preferring taxicabs to subway trains and fancy nightclubs to ordinary restaurants. Yet, in spite of his wealth, Holden is an extremely confused and unhappy young man who, as it quickly becomes apparent, is unable to purchase higher self-esteem.

While Holden is quite fixated on money, he is well aware, on an unconscious level, that money cannot buy him love or higher self-esteem. Throughout the novel, Salinger takes special care to have his character size up his surroundings, his friends, his family and his situation in general in monetary terms. The love, support, and attention which Jem and Scout have come to expect from their father, Atticus, in *To Kill a Mockingbird*, are nowhere evidenced in *The Catcher in the Rye*. The only real love Holden receives comes from his little sister, Phoebe. Unfortunately, she is powerless to solve his problems. In *The Catcher in The Rye*, Salinger does not discount the idea that SES has an important impact upon self-esteem. He does, however, challenge the notion that there is always a positive correlation between SES and self-esteem. . . .

The Outsiders places great emphasis on SES and continuously draws a positive correlation between SES and self-esteem level. The foundation of the novel is predicated upon the conflict between two rival gangs of youths, the "greasers" and the "Socs." (It is interesting to note that Hinton capitalizes the "S" in "Socs" throughout the book while the "g" in greaser is invariably lower case.) The most striking difference between these two groups is that the greasers come from low SES families while the Socs are from high SES families. Numerous comparisons throughout the novel have a direct bearing on the positive correlation between SES and self-esteem level.

While describing Dallas, a fellow gang member, the main character in the novel, Ponyboy, early on expresses his feelings about being a member of a low SES group.

> And you can't win against them [Socs] no matter how hard you try because they've got all the breaks and even whipping them isn't going to change that fact. Maybe that was why Dallas was so bitter.

Not only is Dallas bitter about the Socs, he is bitter about a system that ranks him at the bottom. Only three pages later, Ponyboy manifests this attitude while thinking about girls.

> Still, lots of times I wondered what other girls [not greaser girls] were like. The girls who were bright-eyed and had their dresses a decent length and acted as if they'd like to spit on us if given the chance.

Ponyboy is initially impressed by the Socs, who have Mustangs and Corvairs, and until he meets Cherry Valance, one of the Soc girls, he figures that the Socs have all the advantages. It is through his interaction with Cherry that he realizes the Socs also have problems in spite of their high SES. Unfortunately, as a consequence of this and other discoveries, Ponyboy is the exception to the rule in a scenario dominated by SES. This is a fact which becomes clearer as the novel progresses. Because he is more academically minded than his peers, Ponyboy is able to judge seemingly intractable situations in a more objective manner. His sense of self-esteem is not wholly predicated upon his SES, as is the case with most of his peers, but in some measure upon his academic abilities and insight. He is therefore able to act as a bridge between the greasers and the Socs and foster a reconciliation between the two groups at the novel's close. Ponyboy recognizes, with Cherry's help, that people can relate to one another on terms other than SES—that self-esteem does not have to be solely a function of SES. In this way, he becomes the novel's hero.

Novels in Socioeconomic Terms

[A.] Stern and [D.] Soaring [in 1976] proposed that adolescents, as they become more fully aware of their "social environment," learn that a "stratification system" applies to them as well as others. "They thus gather information about variations in speech, dress, and residence and report uneasiness in encounters with people from different backgrounds, preferring instead class homogeneous social relationships. In this way, stratification knowledge can reduce ambiguity, minimize surprise and help avoid discomfort in everyday life." Given this observation, identification with certain characters in adolescent literature based on their SES would seem both logical and natural. Although all but one of the primary characters in each of the four novels can be placed, in today's terms, at the middle to low end of the SES scale, what is most important is

Greaser Dallas Winston (Matt Dillon) flirts with Soc girls Cherry Valance (Diane Lane) and Marcia (Michelle Meyrink) in the 1983 film version of S.E. Hinton's The Outsiders. © Sunset Boulevard/Corbis.

the way each character perceives his/her own position with respect to SES. Some of the characters are unaware that disparities in SES may result in disparity in self-esteem, as suggested by Jem and Scout in *To Kill a Mockingbird*, while others are keenly cognizant of the way other members of their society interpret and judge them, as in *The Outsiders*. When an adolescent reader identifies with a character, this identification is often of a very personal nature. SES can and often does play an important role in the bonding between character and reader. Attributing a particular SES to his/her character is an important way for an author to enhance the reader's perception of the character as a realistic human being, one with whom the reader can form a strong identification. . . .

Ponyboy, in *The Outsiders*, . . . is at the lower end of the SES scale. He has grown up hating and resenting those of higher SES, but has in some way vindicated himself by achieving the status of scholar among his peers, which he recognizes may one day lead him to a brighter future and higher SES. "We're poorer than the Socs and the middle class," he acknowledges, easily identifying himself with those of low SES. ". . . I'm supposed to be smart; I make good grades and have a high IQ and everything. . . ." Ponyboy is the archetypal underdog, the misfit member of an undeserved low caste. This circumstance alone would be reason enough for many adolescent readers to have a positive identification with him, but his attractiveness goes beyond this. He, like John and Lorraine in *The Pigman*, is able to transcend his position in life—to understand that there are many ways to judge a person other than by SES. His relationship with Cherry Valence, the Soc female, bears out this ability. Cherry says, "You read a lot, don't you Ponyboy? I'll bet you watch sunsets too." In response to her queries, Ponyboy reflects, "It seemed funny to me that the sunset she saw from her patio and the one I saw from the back steps was the same one. Maybe the two worlds we lived in weren't so different. We saw the same sunset."

Ultimately, this ability to see beyond his SES is what enables him to function as a character with whom adolescent readers from a wide range of SESs can identify.

An Effective Learning Device

SES and the awareness of SES stratification function as effective learning devices, providing a means for adolescents to compare themselves to their peers and society as a whole. According to Stern and Searing, "Before leaving secondary school, most adolescents are well aware that society is differentiated between the 'haves' and the 'have-nots.' They are [members of] families with class concepts and are capable of applying them to their immediate situation. They collect information about variations in speech, dress, and residence and recognize differences between blue- and white-collar workers. In this way, adolescence awakens social awareness and permits youths to anticipate experiences in the actual world."

The authors of adolescent literature recognize these ideas and use them to express their own values. What adolescent readers learn in much of today's adolescent literature is that judging others solely on the basis of SES is not only wrong, it is unrealistic. They learn that accepting the reality of a society stratified into SES groups is not only an artificial way of perceiving reality, it is also harmful. Critical to these authors' reasonings is that adolescents' attitudes toward their place in society are still open, and they can be influenced regarding the role of SES in shaping—or not shaping—their lives. The heroes and heroines of adolescent novels are characters who revolt against the prevailing adult order and are able to transcend SES positions, thereby finding meaning and self-actualization in their own values. . . .

In *The Outsiders,* the reader learns that even "greasers" of low SES can be respected by the community for their heroism. John, Ponyboy, and Dallas prove this to be true when they all work together to save a group of schoolchildren from a burning church. The three greasers present a poignant example that there are other ways to achieve recognition and honor.

The Outsiders Reinforces the Existing Social Order

Eric L. Tribunella

Eric L. Tribunella teaches children's and young adult literature at the University of Southern Mississippi. He is the author of many scholarly articles as well as the book Melancholia and Maturation: The Use of Trauma in American Children's Literature.

Tribunella argues in the following viewpoint that The Outsiders, *rather than challenging the status quo of class division in the United States, actually reinforces it.* The Outsiders *at first appears very progressive. It clearly highlights class conflict (in which middle- and upper-class youths abuse lower working-class boys without any real risk of punishment) and demonstrates how these class distinctions harm both Greasers and Socs, who are trapped in their social roles. Tribunella wonders how such a seemingly radical novel has become ensconced in American public schools. He ultimately argues that the book is really an endorsement of the status quo and essentially sabotages its own message.*

In 2001 *Publisher's Weekly* reported that S.E. Hinton's *The Outsiders* ranked second in its list of all-time bestselling children's paperbacks, behind only E.B. White's *Charlotte's Web*. Its relative longevity is fueled no doubt by its frequent inclusion on summer reading lists and its widespread use in secondary school classrooms. This raises the question of why the novel has attained such a prominent place in the canon of instructional fiction. Given that this is a novel written for

Eric L. Tribunella, "Institutionalizing The Outsiders: YA Literature, Social Class, and the American Faith in Education," *Children's Literature in Education*, vol. 38, June 13, 2007, pp. 87–90, 94. Copyright © 2006 by Springer. All rights reserved. Reproduced with kind permission from Springer Science+Business Media and the author.

young adults by a teenager frustrated with the failure of literature to represent the "grittier" elements of adolescence, it
might be surprising that it is now safely ensconced on ap-
proved reading lists for schools throughout the United States.
This fact signals its endorsement by the very adults who embody authority and establishment. What is it about the novel
that lends it to this kind of cultural legitimacy and institu-
tionalization? Educators such as Ann Wilder and Alan B. Tea-
sley suggest that *The Outsiders* was introduced into secondary
schools merely because of its simple language and plot, its
usefulness in exploring the conventions of the novel, its ac-
ceptably sanitary references to sex and violence, or its presum-
able appeal to young adults. These factors alone, however, are
not sufficient to account for why Hinton's novel has resonated
so powerfully in American culture and with American educators. I propose that the educational canonization of *The Outsiders* is enabled in part by the fact that, although it tantalizes
audiences with the relatively rare acknowledgement of social
class as a problem, the novel offers a safe and undisruptive
palliative for class inequality and the endemic malaise of modernity. Its domestication on school reading lists suggests
something about the blunted edge of its class critique. I investigate here how the novel works to contain its own radical potential in this regard, thereby enabling it to be absorbed readily
into educational curricula. . . .

A Tale of Class Conflict

First, we have to clarify the problems depicted in the novel in
order to understand the novel's response to them. The central
conflict in the novel takes shape between two rival groups.
Greasers have long hair, dress in jeans, and have reputations
for being thugs. Their clothes, their reputations, and even the
designation "Greasers" mark their "inferior" class status presumably because the ragged quality of their clothes, for instance, results directly from their poverty. Their rivals are

called "Socs" as shorthand for "the Socials, the jet set, the West-side rich kids." *The Outsiders* represents a clash between conflicting models of youth—on the one hand a nineteenth century and Depression-era model of the child as a necessary economic contributor to the household, and on the other hand the new teenager of the mid-twentieth century whose primary job is going to school and spending money on youth culture. According to Thomas Hine, 26% of boys between the ages of 10 and 15 were employed in paying jobs in 1900, and this did not even include those working on family farms and not receiving wages. [T.] Hine explains that "if you were in your teens during the second half of the nineteenth century, you would likely have been, in one sense, more 'grown up' than either your immediate predecessors or contemporary teenagers. If you were not among the majority of teens on farms, you would more than likely have been working for wages at an adult job to help support the family." Teenage Greasers like Darry and Sodapop, who work to support the family while not attending school, more closely resemble this earlier model. The Socs, with their fancy cars and Madras shirts, are more like the contemporary teenager. The novel, then, represents not simply the conflict between two class positions, but the tensions that emerge from overlapping models of youth shaped by economic trends. The class position of the Greasers is doubly galling, since they suffer not only the difficulties of economic lack, but also the frustration of seeing some of their same-age peers more fully embody the ideals and privileges of the new teenager. . . .

The class status of the Curtis boys makes them particularly vulnerable to the experience of alienation. . . . These vulnerabilities, along with the family's financial difficulties and Darry's physically demanding work as a roofer, undermine the intimacy and affection of the relationship between Darry and Ponyboy. At one point Ponyboy thinks, "Darry thought I was just another mouth to feed and somebody to holler at. Darry love me? I thought of those hard, pale, eyes. . . . Darry doesn't love anyone or anything, except maybe Soda. I didn't hardly think of him as being a human being. I don't care, I lied to myself, I don't care about him either." It is clear that the strain of supporting his two brothers radically affects Darry's mood and bearing because of his physical and emotional fatigue. Ponyboy describes him a bit later in nearly the same terms: "He's hard as a rock and about as human. He's got eyes exactly like frozen ice. He thinks I'm a pain in the neck. He likes Soda—everybody likes Soda—but he can't stand me. I bet he wishes he could stick me in a home somewhere, and he'd do it, too, if Soda'd let him." It is clear that the brothers experience estrangement and unease as a result of their circumstances, which have repercussions for their physical and emotional health. Ponyboy repeatedly describes Darry, who works two jobs, as looking older than his years and as having more worries than he should; he identifies with Pip from Dickens's *Great Expectations* because he can relate to feeling "lousy" about not being a gentleman; and he wonders about the Soc girls who shun and fear him and his Greaser friends.

This condition also afflicts the other youths in the novel, and both Greasers and Socs are left to confront the apparently unbridgeable gulf between the two classes. All of the youths experience varying degrees of anger and resentment because of their class status, about which they are keenly aware, and this is true for the Socs as well. Cherry Valence confesses to Ponyboy the habitual insincerity and dissatisfaction that leaves her and her friends feeling numb: "We're sophisticated—cool to the point of not feeling anything. Nothing is real with us. You know, sometimes I'll catch myself talking to a girl-friend, and realize I don't mean half of what I'm saying." She concludes that these are symptoms of having too much, but not of what can actually fulfill or satisfy: "Did you ever hear of having more than you wanted? So that you couldn't want anything else and then started looking for something else to want?

It seems like we're always searching for something to satisfy us, and never finding it." The feelings expressed here are too sophisticated, sincere, and complex to be dismissed as the harmone-driven turbulence of adolescence. Nor are the feelings of either Greasers or Socs that Hinton manages to articulate even particular to adolescents. Cherry is identifying precisely what social theorists like Charles Taylor have described as the malaise of modernity: a vague discontentment, a sense of unreality, an inability to identify what one wants or needs, a loss of a sense of purpose and significance. Clearly, both Greasers and Socs suffer under the prevailing conditions of their society. In some ways, the conflicts between the two groups distracts from the ways both are caught up in a system that adversely affects both of them.

Both Are Trapped

These youths . . . have the sense that their situations are inescapable. During the climactic rumble between the two groups, Darry confronts Paul Holden, a Soc who had been on the high school football team with him and who has had the opportunity to go to college. Darry has had to give up on college in order to support his two younger brothers. When Ponyboy sees them face off, he realizes that the two young men hate each other because of this difference: "They shouldn't hate each other . . . I don't hate the Socs any more . . . they shouldn't hate . . . [ellipses in original]." Ponyboy is unable to complete the thought. They *shouldn't* hate each other, but he's not sure why, or how to get past that hate. At the moment he has this thought, the first punch in the rumble is thrown, which attests to the hopelessness of altering this mutual animosity. Randy, a Soc, confronts Ponyboy with the purposelessness of the rumble. He plans to skip out on it, despite the ramifications to his reputation, because he is tired of the violence:

Emilio Estevez (Two-Bit), Rob Lowe (Sodapop), Thomas C. Howell (Ponyboy), Patrick Swayze (Darry), and Tom Cruise (Steve) in the 1983 film version of S.E. Hinton's novel The Outsiders. © Sunset Boulevard/Corbis.

I'm sick of it because it doesn't do any good. You can't win, you know that, don't you? . . .You can't win even if you whip us. You'll still be where you were before—at the bottom. And we'll still be the lucky ones with all the breaks. So it doesn't do any good, the fighting and the killing. It doesn't prove a thing. We'll forget it if you win, or if you don't. Greasers will still be greasers and Socs will still be Socs.

Ponyboy does not dispute this observation. He thinks that he would help Randy if he could, but he also recognizes that there is nothing he can do. The rumble will go on, and little will be settled because the economic conditions that underlie the Soc-Greaser conflict will remain unchanged. This recognition is echoed when Ponyboy finally confronts Cherry about her relationship with Bob, the boy Johnny kills while defending himself and Ponyboy. Cherry thinks she's helping by passing news to the Greasers about her Soc friends, but Ponyboy criticizes her. "Do you think your spying for us makes up for the fact that you're sitting there in a Corvette while my brother drops out of school to get a job?" he asks her.

These characters also show evidence of a deep sadness about the separation between Greasers and Socs. When Darry faces off against his former football teammate, Ponyboy detects some expression behind both of their eyes that he cannot quite place. He thinks it might be contempt or pity in the eyes of Paul, and jealousy and shame in Darry's, but their initial hesitancy when confronting each other reveals the possibility of something else: "He looked at Darry and said quietly, 'Hello, Darrel.' Something flickered behind Darry's eyes and then they were ice again. 'Hello, Paul.'" This confrontation, which requires them to engage in violence with each other, is a tragic one. Their quiet hellos, their use of first names, and the fact that they used to "buddy it around all the time," as Ponyboy recalls, suggest as much. Darry and Paul are compelled to meet this way, but it seems likely that what Ponyboy detects behind their eyes is a desire to be buddying it around instead. They must also recognize the impossibility of doing just that. The evidence of their alienation and malaise is clear. While these processes have the potential to affect anyone adversely, irrespective of class status—we see this is the case with Cherry and the Socs—,it is the working class, to which the Greasers belong, who are perhaps least equipped to defend against or resist economic exploitation and state intrusion. One of the qualities of the *The Outsiders* that no doubt fuels its popularity is the ways it calls attention to precisely this vulnerability, which is no doubt experienced to varying degrees by the novel's diverse readership. To the extent that *The Outsiders* is a "problem novel," these, and not merely the fact of physical violence, are the problems it represents, and these collective, systemic problems are bigger than the lives of these particular young adults.

Raising Awareness as a Solution

How, then, does the novel attempt to respond to or manage these problems? What kind of solution does it offer to them? The answers to these questions might point to reasons for why the novel was so readily institutionalized as part of the YA [young adult] canon in American secondary schools. I am arguing that part of the reason for this is that it offers a palliative to the problems associated with social class. Rather than radically challenging, calling into question, or disrupting the social systems and processes that produce, contribute to, or sustain those problems, the novel achieves a kind of sleight of hand: in representing those problems it seems to be offering solutions to them, but the solutions it offers—the representation and knowledge of the problem itself—cannot be seen as constituting adequate or successful responses. In other words, *The Outsiders* is not a terribly threatening novel; therefore, it is able to be listed safely on school reading lists without raising any serious flags about radical social reform or revolution. Of course, a novel is by no means required (by whom or how would it be required anyway?) to offer solutions to social problems, but the point is that the novel represents itself, or at least Ponyboy represents it, as precisely this kind of intervention. Let me be clear. I am not offering a moral or aesthetic evaluation of the novel and its political project; rather, I am attempting to explain how the novel represents itself as a critique of social class while at the same time it undermines its own purported agenda. We can, therefore, consider how this intervention works.

As the novel concludes, Johnny and Dallas are dead and the rift between Greasers and Socs continues even if there is a temporary cessation of group violence. Ponyboy sits down to complete his late English assignment, and what he composes turns out to be the novel itself. The idea to write about his experiences for his English class is prompted by the fact that it is too late to tell Dallas that there is "still lots of good in the world." If he cannot tell Dallas, then he decides to tell others:

> Suddenly it wasn't only a personal thing to me. I could picture hundreds and hundreds of boys living on the wrong side of cities, boys with black eyes who jumped at their own

shadows. Hundreds of boys who maybe watched sunsets and looked at stars and ached for something better. I could see boys going down under street lights because they were mean and tough and hated the world, and it was too late to tell them that there was still good in it, and they wouldn't believe you if you did. It was too vast a problem to be just a personal thing. There should be some help, someone should tell them before it was too late. Someone should tell their side of the story, and maybe people would understand then and wouldn't be so quick to judge a boy by the amount of hair oil he wore. It was important to me.

This, then, is the response of both Ponyboy and the novel to the problems described above. This response takes the form of a textual narrative. The way Ponyboy articulates this impulse and its rationale is telling. He begins with the recognition that the problem is not merely a personal one, and hundreds of other boys exist out in the world who share the problems of himself and his friends. This is a broader, social issue he is considering. The form of that response has a dual function. It can work as an instance of personal catharsis, and it can represent and communicate more broadly the fact of the problem itself. In the first case, the catharsis of Ponyboy or the reader who experiences it vicariously is precisely an individual response. It might help Ponyboy process his traumatic experiences and ground his emotional recovery, but this individual catharsis does not itself address or intervene in the larger social processes at work to produce or sustain the problem of class inequality and alienation. . . .

Education as a Remedy

The question is: what sense or impression might readers take from *The Outsiders*? The stark image of the concluding pages, irrespective of Ponyboy's reference to "hundreds and hundreds of boys," is that of the figure of the individual, fictive author (Ponyboy), working alone to compose his personal account. This conclusion, inadvertently or not, advocates a kind of rugged individualism in the face of systemic, even epochal, social problems, while suggesting that what Ponyboy desires is the well-being of all boys like himself, that is, the interests of the community. It is that slippage I am interested in. The figure of the solitary author-hero presides over the novel, and this solitary act is his ultimate response to the problems and traumas he has confronted. Nevertheless, those problems, and the systems and processes that (re)produce them, require a collective response if any attempt is going to be made to resist or repair them. The novel at its conclusion elevates the figure of the individual, heroic, authorial survivor and elides the gang, except as an audience, yet this is precisely the moment when the collective and communal quality of their lives might be mobilized against those very problems.

The conclusion of the novel, its revelation of itself as the product of an instructional assignment, ultimately suggests the course of action endorsed in response to the problems it depicts. This conclusion effectively reaffirms a liberal faith in education. Ponyboy's response to his traumatic experiences, which are symptomatic of problems of social class and class inequality, is to do his homework. His sensitivity and insight is channeled into an educational pursuit, and the implication is that Ponyboy, perhaps more so than his Greaser buddies, is a good boy, good citizen, and most importantly, good student. Unlike Darry or Sodapop, who have dropped out of school, Ponyboy will eventually escape or transcend some of the problems of the Greasers by getting a good education. And this might work for Ponyboy, whom the reader gathers is capable of being studious—we might even say that he is "college bound"—but we are left to wonder about Greasers like Two-Bit or like Sodapop, who confesses to Ponyboy that he was never very good at school. Meanwhile, Socs like Paul and Randy are on track to maintain their status as the social elite by going to college, but Cherry has already suggested that they are far from immune to the problems of alienation and malaise. In fact, the pursuit or maintenance of this status, within a particular social-economic system, might itself be what Cherry finds so toxic.

Education Perpetuates Class Conflict

In *The Imperfect Panacea*, historian of education Henry Perkinson argues that the conceptualization of education in the U.S. as a solution to every major social problem is fundamentally misguided. . . .

Perkinson clarifies the flaw in logic that underlies this faith in education: "the notion that the school was a panacea for all of society's problems carried with it the assumption that people were the root of the problem: *they* had to be changed; never the existing arrangements, *never* the system." *The Outsiders* plays on precisely this confusion. After establishing the problems associated with social class—systemic and generational inequality, alienation and malaise—the novel concludes by offering what it represents as a possible solution to that problem: Ponyboy's education and individualism. The point is that, as Perkinson suggests, this solution is not really a solution. It involves the transformation of Ponyboy, but not the transformation of the system, as socialization involves transforming people, not social structures or processes. Moroever, education as socialization can also work to inculcate in the student certain sets of assumptions and certain ways of thinking—not just simply knowledge itself, but whole systems of thought that enable and constrain what it is possible to know or not know—that make it *more* difficult to recognize and respond to social problems and what sustains them. Put simply, if through education we learn that what it takes to solve the problem of social class is to work hard, get a good education, and attain middle-class respectability, then that education has worked to mystify rather than clarify how social class and inequality work and how one might act in ways to alter the social order. This is what I am suggesting *The Outsiders* does. . . .

Endorsing the Status Quo

I began with the question of why *The Outsiders* has been folded so comfortably into secondary school curricula, the very purpose of which is precisely the maintenance and reproduction of the social order. My answer is that the novel is effectively an endorsement of American education and that the obfuscations of the novel work to mystify further the problems it seems to expose. It does this by representing itself as a solution, thereby obstructing inquiry rather than prompting it, which it achieves through a conclusion that constructs the novel as a closed circuit. It ends where it begins, and it elevates the work of the solitary author-hero over and above the collaboration of the collective. Its widespread educational use has the capacity to function as the containment of a potentially oppositional text within the domesticating and deradicalizing context of the official school curriculum. What I am calling an obfuscation is indeed consistent with one of the central lessons of the novel: Johnny's exhortation to "stay gold," or remain childlike, where to be childlike is understood as meaning innocent, unknowing, and naïve. This novel represents a faith in educational excellence, but the reader must not forget, as Ponyboy must not forget, Johnny's warning. If, in fact, this conclusion mystifies rather than clarifies the problems of social class by re-asserting education as a solution when this can only work, if it can be said to work at all, for the exceptional individual, then we must consider the possibility that education itself involves ignorance. Ponyboy is to know some things and not others, and so must the reader. The novel itself works to encourage the reader to remain innocent and unknowing of its own limitations as a solution to the problems of social class, and as long as U.S. culture is invested in the image of children or young adults as innocent and unknowing, *The Outsiders* will continue to be an unproblematized and underachieving mainstay of the high school reading list.

An Alternate Reading: Staying Gold

Ultimately, I want to suggest that this text, as all texts, can be made to do more. Of course, this novel is not a how-to manual for social reform or proletariat revolution; nevertheless, we might consider the text's potential for more liberatory instruction. I have referred repeatedly to what I call the novel's sleight of hand. One effect of magic tricks is that they tend to inspire the question, "How'd you do that?" That is, the very success of the trick promotes a suspicious investigation into precisely how the trick works. Here, perhaps, is the potential of *The Outsiders* to provoke a more oppositional reading that resists the palliative and enervating uses of literature in education. To the extent that we imagine successful maturation as involving the achievement of a sense of adult responsibility, and to the extent that getting an education involves preparing young people to be compliant, productive, adult workers, then we might read Johnny's exhortation to "stay gold" as suggesting a resistance to precisely this developmental trajectory. In other words, if becoming an adult means entering the alienating, malaise-inducing, profit-driven world of adult work, then Johnny might be warning Ponyboy not to succumb to the dominant ideology of what it means to be a successful adult in a capitalist society. If this is what Johnny means, it *is* truly radical advice. The conclusion then is more ambiguous than I might have suggested earlier. It leaves the reader with the possibility of a more oppositional reading, even if that oppositional reading is highly circumscribed by a young person's encounter with the text in the context of an institution—the school. It might result, if the reader takes Johnny's advice, in a refusal to take one's place in a system that results in alienation and malaise. Of course, successful resistance itself requires a knowledge and understanding of the problems or systems that need to be resisted, and so education is necessary. A more optimistic reading of Ponyboy's return to his homework might understand him as seeking precisely this education, even if the form of his education might ultimately defeat his purpose. To take from traditional education the tools of resistance is possible, albeit difficult, and success is likely limited only to the most exceptional youth, which is precisely the problem the conclusion of the novel suggests. Again, *The Outsiders* provides no plan of action, and its very implications are obscure and contradictory at best. Still, any text that in some way addresses a systemic social problem might work to motivate the reader to seek more information about the problem, to ask important questions, and to consider alternatives to the outcomes presented in the novel; it might clarify how the problem works, what helps produce and sustain it; and it might provoke an affective response that motivates a coherent, organized, and collective one.

Notes

Taylor, C. (2005), *The Ethics of Authenticity*, Cambridge, Mass: Harvard University Press.

The Outsiders Offers a Nuanced Critique of Class Mobility and Gender Identity

June Pulliam

June Pulliam teaches English and Women's and Gender Studies at Louisiana State University. She is the author of numerous academic articles and books examining popular films and novels, focusing especially on the horror genre.

In the following viewpoint Pulliam explores the nuanced representations of class and gender in S.E. Hinton's The Outsiders. *Specifically, she notes how socioeconomic class frees the Socs— making it possible for them to be destructive without the limits of economic constraints or legal repercussions—and burdens the Greasers both materially, and in that they are more exposed to legal harassment than the Socs. She goes on to argue that the novel's female author portrays gender roles interestingly: While the Socs are confined to their gender roles by the rigid expectations of their class, Johnny and Ponyboy—almost by virtue of their tough greaser image—are free to engage in what would otherwise be unacceptably feminine behavior.*

S.E. Hinton's story of gang rivalry is not wholly original: precursors are found in texts such as William Shakespeare's *Romeo and Juliet* or *West Side Story*, itself loosely based on Shakespeare's play. However, in these narratives, the warring factions are all from similar class backgrounds. *Romeo and Juliet's* Montagues and Capulets are both families of comparable wealth, and *West Side Story's* Sharks and Jets are gangs of working class youth, though they are of different ethnicities (the Sharks are Puerto Rican, while the Jets are white). *The Outsiders'* Socs and Greasers are racially homogenous; instead, they represent warring class factions. The Socs are the wealthy kids from the West Side who drive new cars and wear sweaters and checked madras shirts, cut their hair short and listen to the Beatles, while the Socs are working class boys from the East Side who walk or drive jalopies, wear t-shirts and jeans, slick back their long hair (hence the term Greasers) and listen to Elvis. But these trappings are just the outward manifestations of their identities. Class differences are what really fuels their rancor for one another.

Class Conflict in *The Outsiders*

Class can be defined as the relationship to the means of production. The Socs, with their parents' material wealth, have a much more privileged relationship to the means of production than do the Greasers. The Greasers have far fewer resources to draw upon when they are hit with a crisis. When Ponyboy's parents are killed in a car accident, Darry must give up his dreams of going to college to support his brothers. He is not legally obligated to care for his younger siblings. They could be left to state care. But the state would place his brothers in a group home where they would suffer greatly from a lack of adult attention. And if either Ponyboy or Soda get into trouble with the law, the justice system is quite capable of deciding that Darry is doing a bad job of parenting and remove his brothers from his guardianship. Presumably, if Darry and his brothers were members of the Socs, there might be money in the bank or a life insurance policy to provide a cushion against this type of disaster, or there might even be wealthy relatives who would be willing to help.

The Greasers' and the Socs' animosity for one another is due to prevailing ideas about class, particularly in the United States. To be poor or prosperous are more than just accidents of birth according to this ideology—they are moral categories.

In the United States, children are often taught to believe that class mobility is not just possible, but it is nearly inevitable for anyone who works hard. The [link] between wealth and morality is originally from the Puritans, who believed that material prosperity was evidence that the individual was one of God's elect. These ideas were enshrined in American popular culture through sources such as Horatio Alger's fiction. In Alger's Ragged Dick novels, his protagonist literally rises from rags to riches due to his own tenacity and superior moral nature. So it's not surprising that the Socs see the Greasers as deserving recipients of their violence. For the Socs, their parents and for those who regulate society such as the legal system and the school system, the Greasers are juvenile delinquents with no ambition in life beyond fighting and drinking. Very little thought is given to how the Greasers' lack of wealth combined with class prejudices against them perpetuates their membership in this category. Also note that the consequences for delinquency are far less severe for the Socs than they are for the Greasers. The justice system (police, judges, etc.) are predisposed to see Greasers as fundamentally bad and deserving of harsh punishment. For the Socs, the penalties for delinquency are lighter. The justice system is more inclined to see them as good boys who just made uncharacteristically bad choices when they have scuffles with the law, and hence, the penalties are less severe.

Class privilege is further demonstrated by the Socs' preferred method of fighting. It's customary for several of them to jump one Greaser. This not only demonstrates their overall cowardice, but how, in a sense, all of the Greasers will eternally be jumped by the Socs in that the Socs have a more privileged relationship to the means of production and so the two classes can rarely meet one another on an equal footing. Perhaps the reason the Greasers are so desirous of fighting the Socs in a rumble is because this arena of physical violence is the only true meritocracy.

Class Mobility in English Literature

Both Ponyboy's and Johnny's tastes in literature demonstrate how they have internalized ideas of middle and upper class masculinity. Johnny is fascinated with *Gone with the Wind*, a novel more traditionally read by women than by men, because he "was especially stuck on the Southern gentlemen— impressed with their manners and charm." And Ponyboy comments that when he had to read Charles Dickens' *Great Expectations* the character of Pip reminded him of his gang, "the way he felt marked lousy because he wasn't a gentleman or anything, and the way that girl kept looking down on him." Pip, of course, eventually becomes a middle class gentleman, as much through the good fortune of having a secret benefactor who sends him to school and sees that he has opportunities to rise later in life as through hard work. And while the planter class in *Gone with the Wind* is represented as a sort of aristocracy who came into their money, Scarlett O'Hara's and Rhett Butler's parents and grandparents were able to work their way up to this position through a combination of tenacity and very good luck. Scarlett and her other Atlanta neighbors must regain (or lose) that position after the War through more hard work. Johnny's fascination with the manners of the Southern gentleman is also worth noting. When the middle class began to emerge in the 18th century, its members attempted [to] legitimate themselves as something better than nouveau riche by not only aping the consumer purchases [of] titled gentry, but by distinguishing themselves with manners. Before the rise of the middle class, a gentleman was someone with an inherited title, something not available to everyone. After the rise of the middle class, however, a gentleman came to be defined as someone who behaved in a certain way, something that conceivably anyone could do. Plays such as George Bernard Shaw's *Pygmalion* (made into the musical *My Fair Lady*) show how class is not something immutable, but rather, a social construction. If Eliza Doolittle can be taught to convince other social elites that she is a duchess, then class is not genetic.

Gender Identity Among the Greasers

It's made clear immediately that Ponyboy, the story's protagonist, does not embody the stereotypes of working class masculinity. He is not a mindless brawler, but literate and contemplative. He enjoys books and film, and prefers going to the movies alone so that he can better explore the nuances of the story. When Ponyboy tells us about the other Greasers, it is clear that they too don't completely embody this stereotype of working class masculinity, regardless of how they dress or with whom they associate. Collectively, the Greasers are "almost like hoods; [they] steal things and drive old souped-up cars and hold up gas stations and have a gang fight once in a while." Yet this description does not even begin to describe the individual members of the gang that Ponyboy runs with. Two-Bit Matthews, the joker of the gang, "liked fights, blondes, and for some unfathomable reason, school" since he wasn't a particularly good student. Perhaps Dally and Johnny best embody stereotypes of working class family life. Dally is the most hardened member of the bunch: he "spent three years on the wild side of New York and had been arrested at the age of ten", and as a result, was tougher, colder and meaner than the rest of them. Johnny is the weakest and youngest member of the gang, and comes from the sort of family that is normally attributed to people of his class: "His father was always beating him up, and his mother ignored him, except when she was hacked off at something, and then you could hear her yelling at him clear down at our house."

Ponyboy and Johnny have the most ambiguous gender identity of the Greasers, and if it were not for their ability to fight, they would be seen as completely feminine. Both enjoy sunsets and are unashamed to cry in the other's presence, and both enjoy *Gone with the Wind*, a quintessentially feminine narrative. It is also not surprising that characters in a YA [young adult] novel would have ambiguous gender identities given that so many of these narratives are *Entwicklungsromane* [novels of personal development]. After all, these characters are frequently on the verge of forming their gender identities, consciously and unconsciously choosing qualities that they will emulate from those around them, both male and female.

At the end of the novel, the character with the most feminine identity, Johnny, and the character with the most masculine identity, Dally, both die. Perhaps having a gender identity that is not a healthy balance between masculine and feminine, but is instead too heavily weighted in one direction or the other, leads to death. Dally has always felt so little and flirted with danger so much that it is always suicidal. And Johnny feel so much and puts others before himself to such a degree that it would be difficult for him to survive to adulthood either.

Family Among Greasers and Socs

Ponyboy's non-traditional family does not embody negative stereotypes of working class life. His older brother Darry, who is forced to be father and mother to him and his little brother Sodapop since their parents died, might be prosaic in that he "doesn't understand anything that is not plain hard fact. But he uses his head." Sodapop is movie star handsome, but not particularly intellectual. Still, he has a joy of living so keen that he never touches alcohol since he "can get drunk in a drag race or dancing without ever going near alcohol." Ponyboy's parents are also not stereotypical working class brutes either, but instead, were loving and involved in their children's lives. His father was "never rough with anyone without meaning to be," unlike Darry, who has a gruff manner with his younger brothers, mainly because of the pressure of suddenly having to become the sole bread winner and a single father when their parents died in an auto accident. Darry's fate in particular illustrates to what degree class mobility is a myth. Ponyboy thinks of his brother that

> Darry didn't deserve to work like an old man when he was only twenty. He had been a real popular guy in school; he was captain of the football team and he had been voted Boy of the Year. But we just didn't have the money for him to go to college, even with the athletic scholarship he won. And now he didn't have the time between jobs to even think about college.

With no student loan program or no Pell Grants, and no ability to join the military and benefit from the GI Bill when his tour of duty is up (he must care for his minor brothers after all, or they'll be put in a state home), Darry's fate is sealed. Furthermore, there is little hope for Ponyboy since the same forces that have shaped Darry's life are also conspiring to make it extremely difficult for him to leave the working class.

The kids who have the traditional, stable middle class family such as Bob are not necessarily better parented in these situations. Randy says of his deceased best friend Bob (Robert Shelton) that his parents "spoiled him rotten . . . gave into him all the time. [Bob] kept trying to make someone say 'No' and they never did." Ponyboy's non-traditional family is more caring and stable than is Bob's.

Class Differences as Value Differences

Ponyboy meets Cherry Valence, a Soc girl, at the movies one night. Cherry first notices Ponyboy due to the negative attention his friend Dally attracts talking dirty and making a disturbance in order to deliberately annoy the Soc girls. After Cherry tells Dally where to get off, her friend asks Ponyboy and Johnny to come sit with them as protection against further insults. It is under these circumstances that Ponyboy sees the similarities between himself and people of another class (and sex). When Ponyboy tells Cherry the story of the beating

Title page of Horatio Alger's 1967 Ragged Dick *series about an industrious boot black whose rags-to-riches story seems to suggest that poverty is caused by delinquency rather than misfortune.* © Corbis.

that Johnny took nearly four months prior to the novel's opening, she comments that "all Socs aren't like that" and "things are rough all over," for both the Socs and the Greasers.

For Cherry, different values, not money, separate the two groups. She describes the Greasers [as] more emotional, while the Socs are "sophisticated—cool to the point of not feeling anything." Yet Cherry fails to appreciate how these characteristics she assigns to the two groups are also a result of class. She understands that the Socs suffer from having more than they want, and as a result continue to search for some intangible thing to satisfy them, but she fails to understand that this almost spiritual hunger is a function of having all of their basic material needs for food and shelter met. Not having to worry about whether or not they'll be able to eat or have a roof over their heads or can even feel safe walking home at night gives them the leisure to have this longing for the ineffable.

Class and Emotional Volatility

Because Cherry is female, she doesn't get involved in drunken brawls the way her boyfriend does, but she too has her own suicidal impulses. Before she leaves Ponyboy, she comments of Dally that she could fall in love with him. We later learn that Bob, her doomed boyfriend, has the same qualities as Dallas: "he was a reckless, hot-tempered boy, cocky and scared stiff at the same time." And the more emotionally volatile behavior that Cherry assigns to the Greasers is also a result of class (as well as a classist stereotype).

Class training encourages the Socs to be less outwardly emotional than the Greasers. Containing one's emotions represents the ability to control one's self in other arenas in life, and the working class is often characterized as a group lacking self control, hence its lack of money or inability to complete enough education to secure a middle class job. However, this characterization does not take into account the tremendous capital of class privilege—it is much more difficult to go to college and secure a middle class job when one's family lacks the money for school and when other family members haven't previously negotiated this system. The Socs have more agency in their lives than do the Greasers. Both groups of teens might have much in common, but when the Greasers become adults, they have a lot less ability to determine the trajectory of their lives than do their better-off counterparts.

On p. 37, Ponyboy begins to considers how he and Cherry (and by implication other Socs) are similar. But he is not completely convinced that things are rough all over: "things are rough all over, all right. All over the East Side." Johnny's father is an alcoholic and his mother an uncaring shrew; Two-bit's mother works in a bar to support her children after being deserted by their father; Darry gets old before his time trying to support his two younger brothers, and Sodapop drops out of school to help him support Ponyboy. Meanwhile, "the Socs had so much spare time and money that they jumped us and each other for kicks, had beer blasts and river-bottom parties because they didn't know what else to do."

Gender Roles as a Function of Class

The female characters in this novel are secondary. Cherry Valence, Bob's girlfriend and the Soc spy that the Greasers have before the war, is like a good many middle class girls of her age, then and now. Cherry has been raised to remain relatively aloof with boys, and this has given her a sense of her own self worth. We see this when she doesn't hesitate to tell off Dally when he talks dirty to her, or later when we discover that she and her girlfriend have left their middle class boyfriends for the night because they've been drinking and presumably, have been behaving unacceptably as a consequence. And she is willing to spy for the [greasers] because she realizes that what Bob did was wrong. But she is also a creature of her particular historical time. Cherry falls in love with Bob, and fears she could fall in love with Dally as well, because she is attracted to these sorts of "bad boy" men. Cherry's attraction to dangerous men is not unique, but something women are often programmed by their culture to do. The attraction to the dangerous man is part of the Ur [German term connoting primordial and basic] myth of the power of "true" femininity to be able to change a man's worst flaws. We see this myth replayed in stories such as "Beauty and the Beast," where Belle's love for the beast transforms him into a handsome gentleman with better manners. This myth not only gives women the dangerous idea that they can change a man's bad (and sometimes dangerous habits), but that furthermore, it is their responsibility to do so. Such an idea is particularly dangerous when a woman becomes involved with an abusive partner; the myth causes her to believe that she can change the abusive behavior and often leads her to stay in a violent relationship rather than flee. Note that Cherry is attracted to "bad boys" from both sides of the tracks too, so her ability to fall in love with Dally is more than just a fascination with someone coming from a different class background.

Most of the main characters in this novel are male, and the author is female. Furthermore, with the exception of characters such as Bob, Dally and Darry, most don't fall into stereotypical patterns of masculinity, but can be nurturing and sensitive as well. Can we read this as a female author attempting to make male characters, particularly the bad boy characters, who might be worth someone like Cherry falling in love with?

Risk, Identity, and Transcending Class

When Johnny, Dally and Ponyboy discover that the church is on fire, Dally wants everyone to stay put, but Johnny and Ponyboy instinctively run to see what's the matter and go into the church to rescue the children, at great peril to themselves. Later, the three are lauded as heroes, but don't get much else for their efforts. Johnny's young life is cut short, and really death is the best option for him given the injuries he's sustained in the fire. "Even if Johnny did live he'd be crippled and never play football or help us out in a rumble again. He'd have to stay in that house he hated, where he wasn't wanted, and things could never be like they used to be." And Ponyboy is so consumed by grief over Johnny's death that he begins to claim that he, not Johnny, killed Bob as a way of denying that his friend is dead. And Dally, who doesn't have any family, is so filled with grief over Johnny's death that he commits suicide by cop. And the entire incident has brought Ponyboy's family situation to the attention of the authorities, who are now investigating whether or not Darry is a fit parent for his younger brothers. Yet helping others is important. It gives Johnny and Ponyboy some momentary agency to do good, and this agency is a powerful feeling. Ponyboy notices of Johnny when he dashes into the burning church that [that] "was the only time I can think of when I saw him without that defeated, suspicious look in his eyes. He looked like he was having the time of his life."

At the end of the novel, the writer's hand is revealed (the fictional writer, anyway) when it becomes clear that Ponyboy is telling his story in an essay for his English teacher which will help him get a passing grade in that class. Yet this narrative serves a far greater function than merely letting him get a "C" in English. It also permits him to construct his self, viewing his experience during this short period of time as one that has forever transformed him into the man he will become. It is also significant that Ponyboy is putting his experience into narrative form since we make sense of the world through telling stories. All religious traditions have narratives of creation that explain our purpose in the world, nations have narratives of their founding that are sort of like mission statements, letting the world know who they collectively think they are. And individuals construct narratives to explain who they are by means of connecting their identities to a coherent string of past events that clearly point to the present. For example, a victim of child sexual abuse might, through therapy, come to comprehend what happened to her, and subsequently form a narrative about the abuse and its connection to her present life that helps her understand how she has been affected, and hopefully heal as a result. By writing his story, Ponyboy is similarly attempting to make sense of things that happened to him that are beyond his comprehension until they can be put into narrative form.

Opulence to Decadence: *The Outsiders* and *Less Than Zero*

Ellen A. Seay

Ellen A. Seay is an experienced classroom teacher and critic of adolescent literature.

In the following selection Seay compares S.E. Hinton's The Outsiders—*which was written in the 1960s and largely lacks graphic language, sex, and violence—with Bret Easton Ellis's* Less Than Zero *(1985), a novel steeped in violence, profanity, and morally ambiguous sex. What Seay finds most notable is that, while the novels are extremely different—beyond their differing aesthetics, Hinton focuses on notions of nobility and social class demonstrated in the division between greasers and Socs, while Ellis constructs a decadent universe entirely populated by wealthy, nihilistic Socs—both entirely lack an adult world of authority, protection, or mentorship. These novels make literal what many adolescents feel: That adults are entirely out of the loop, neither guiding teens toward self-realization, nor protecting them from a hostile world or their own bad judgment.*

"The times, they are a-changin'." Bob Dylan sang it back in the 1960s, and it was a particularly applicable message in those turbulent times. Adolescent literature has ridden the crest of change in the last twenty years, just like adult fiction. Fiction for juveniles no longer gives us virginal Sally worrying about whether or not John will give her his class ring at the senior prom. It was fun and it was mindless, and certainly several generations of boys and girls were not harmed by what they read. Life in general was wonderful if you worked hard, studied hard and drank your milk. The rewards of these endeavors were a good job, a good spouse, nice children, a frame house, a dog and a paneled station wagon. What more could any nice, young, white, middle-class American teenager want?

What they wanted, eventually, was reality. And they got it. Of course, there are those who will argue that they have gotten too much, too soon. But, unquestionably, adolescent fiction has caught up with the adult demand for truth in literature.

What still varies isn't so much the telling, but what is being told. Surely S.E. Hinton's adolescent classic *The Outsiders* (New York: Viking, 1967) has as much to say about the inherent good in teens as Bret Easton Ellis' recently published *Less Than Zero* (New York: Simon and Schuster, 1985) has to say about all that is bad. While *The Outsiders* is uplifting and positive despite tragic occurrences, the nihilistic *Less Than Zero* offers only the truth of the no hope/no solution Southern California teens of the late 1980s. Despite vast differences between the books, both have been controversial in their own times and both are eerily effective and moving in their own ways.

Briefly, *Zero* chronicles the reentry of Clay, a freshman at a small Ivy League college, into the fast-paced California lifestyle he has left behind. Clay spends his Christmas vacation reexperiencing this lifestyle and examining his place in it.

On the surface, there seems to be little in common between the two books. *The Outsiders* was written twenty years ago by then sixteen-year-old S.E. Hinton. It dealt with the split between the high school social classes in Tulsa, Oklahoma. *Less Than Zero*, written by twenty-year-old Ellis, then a Bennington College undergraduate, takes place in 1986. *Zero*, which is rapidly gathering a cult following, deals with the pursuit of something, anything, meaningful by the eighteen- and nineteen-year-old children of the idly rich of Los Angeles and surrounding affluent areas. The main characters in *The Out-*

siders are poor and on the lower end of the financial and social scale, while their counterparts in *Less Than Zero* define the top of that same scale. The "greasers" in Hinton's novel have nothing but their pride and their desires. Their enemies are the "Socs," the financially well-off teens who live on the other side of town and torment them as a pastime. Ellis' characters have all that one could financially desire: the best cars, the best bars, the best clothes, the best music, the best drugs. Their enemies aren't the poor—they are themselves.

Both stories deal with violence, but it is a different kind of violence. In *The Outsiders*, Ponyboy and Johnny flee into the country when Johnny stabs and kills Bob in self-defense. The inevitable gang fight is set up to settle the score. The characters in Hinton's novel deal in various levels of physical violence to compensate for their lack of things: lack of respect, lack of money, lack of stature, lack of a visibly bright future. They fight in their various ways: Two-Bit's pride and joy is a fancy black-handled switchblade; Steve and Darry are both into building their physiques; Tim Shepard and his gang slash tires and beat up people for the hell of it; and Dallas rolls drunks, fights, and in the end, dies after sticking up a store in frustration and rage. The message in some way seems to be that those who live by violence will die by it in the same degree.

But while violence in *The Outsiders* is intensely real in its physical manifestations, the violence in *Less Than Zero*, although not physical, is equally devastating. We are used to dealing with violence as a physical concept: beatings, shootings, stabbings, or other bodily damage. But what about the violence to one's mind? Seemingly, in the twenty years between the two novels, the violence has turned inward.

The mental violence of *Less Than Zero* occurs for a variety of reasons. What is questionable is whether it occurs because of outside influences or whether the characters, in their search for excitement and stimulation, do it to themselves. The main character, Clay, forces himself in horror and fascination to watch his childhood friend, Julian, willingly commit a number of homosexual acts for money. Society generally views homosexuality negatively as something of a perversion. Yet Clay's quest for excitement has led him to cast aside societal mores, and he enters into a horror world, a counter world to what society sees as normal. He sleeps with an acquaintance, Griffin, and is seemingly unaffected by the incident. He snorts an abundance of cocaine and attends parties where his friends are in some way or another messed up. Their problems have no meaning for him, and his life is equally meaningless to his friends. They don't question him about anything other than surface matters unless he appears to be breaking out of the quest-for-desire mold that they all live in.

All this contributes to a collapse within Clay's mind. Everything around him is opulent, and yet decadent, with outside influences no doubt contributing to his downfall. The cocaine, the fancy cars, the beautiful and rich males and females, the free sex, and the endless supply of money that can purchase all of the above are the weapons that he turns upon himself. In the midst of absolute riches, he can find nothing worth thinking about or working for. The opulence does its violence upon him in that he becomes one of the mindless. Apparently, this is the only way he can save himself.

But ultimately, he does have control. In the end, his abuse of all around him is his own choice. The violence that results within his mind kills part of him, just as surely as the policeman's bullet kills Dallas Winston. The two of them are alike in that the violence done to them comes from outside factors. And yet both of them willingly brought it upon themselves in a desperate effort to gain control, in some way, of their lives.

While the differences between these two books are obvious, there are many subtle ways that they are alike. Both deal with an unwanted faction of society. The greasers are loved by no one but their own and are generally feared and despised. While abusing them and beating them up, the Soc's fear the greasers, as do the nurses in the hospital and the newspapermen who cover Johnny and Ponyboy's story. While the other factions of society reject the greasers, the rejection of the teens in *Less Than Zero* is a bit more subliminal. Author Ellis never comes out and says that they are hated, or despised. If anything, they are probably idolized by the less fortunate who wish they were as well off.

Yet the rejection and the labeling of these characters as an unwanted faction of society is there. It is not the other characters in the story who do the rejecting; it is the reader. We reject them as worthless because of their self-absorption. We reject them because of the almost non-human way that they deal with each other and the world. Their lack of feelings and emotions repels us. And we are particularly critical of them because they have everything; the world is an open door, and they have all of the keys. Yet they wallow in their pettiness and never use the opportunities that they have had handed to them to do anything that could be called ethically worthwhile.

There is a marked absence of parenting as we know it in both *The Outsiders* and *Less Than Zero*. In Hinton's novel, the parents are apparently dead, nonexistent or not around. But Darry acts as a sort of parent for Ponyboy and Soda after their parents are killed in an auto accident. He sacrifices college opportunities so that he may work and keep what is left of his family together. He monitors Ponyboy's reading material and is constantly on him about his schoolwork. He sets curfews and even tries to get Soda and Ponyboy to eat right. Yet Darry is not the parent. If anything, he is the model of what most teenagers want: a parent who is both strict and understanding. He exhibits parental ways, yet he is a friend as well. By most teenagers' standards, parents cannot be friends.

In *Less Than Zero* there are parents, but for all practical purposes, there might as well not be any. Their function in the lives of their children seems to be limited to providing the necessities of life: food, shelter, cable TV. They are consumed in their own lives and what attention they pay to their children is almost perfunctory. Clay's father asks him what he wants for Christmas: how about renewing his subscription to "Variety"? As a substitute for real conversation, these parents buy their children material things because they believe this is all that is demanded or required of them. One of Clay's friends, Kim, never seems to know where her mother is and finds out by reading the gossip columns in some of the trade rags. She isn't overly concerned; she only wants to know so that she will be able to answer the question when someone asks her.

Both of these books are striking examples of adolescent literature and the extremes to which it has gone. Both tell effective and haunting stories. Both make points that are well taken and succeed in opening our eyes. But the similarities end there.

Hinton's novel contains no sex, no graphic physical violence, and no bad or offensive language. Yet the novel was a success without those elements and is considered a minor teenage classic. The time in which it was written may have dictated that these elements not be contained in the book; but even so, it really doesn't need them to succeed. Adding sex, gore and bad language would have changed the scope and tone of *The Outsiders* and probably would have focused unnecessary attention on those aspects. If anything, their inclusion in the story may have taken away from it. In the same way, taking out the sex, gore and language in *Less Than Zero* would have severely diminished the message. It is devastating because of the dealings with those very things, and the characters are what they are because of their deep involvement in all of these. Their dealings with the dark side of life are what make them, and the story, what it is.

What can be learned from *Less Than Zero* far outweighs the inclusion of sex, violence, homosexuality, drug abuse and all the other dark elements that make up the book. Few readers want to experience the anguish of Clay, trapped in an exclusive *Alice in Wonderland* setting. What they want to do is wish that he could see beyond his gilded cage and take advantage of the opportunities that he has. They learn by example what is good and what is bad. There will be a few students who will wish that they had a Jag, all the coke in the world, great clothes and sex with whomever and whenever they want. After all, we've all been taught to work to be rich and if we do so, the rewards will be ours. But those who read further will find that the payoff is not without a price. The price is one's soul, and, for Clay, the payment is due.

The Hinton book is a classic because it deals with the basic tenets of the human spirit: good and evil. While society frowns upon Ponyboy, Dallas and the rest of the greasers, we as readers see that they have much to offer that is positive. Compared to Clay and his cohorts, Ponyboy and the greasers have much. They have a brotherhood, a unity amongst their own for which they are willing to fight. They take care of and are concerned about each other. They are willing to make sacrifices. Dallas gives Johnny and Pony a gun, even though it could mean jail for him. He takes the heat from the police and spends a night in jail so that the police will look elsewhere for the fugitives. Darry gives up his dreams of college to support his brothers. Dallas, although unable to express it, wants Johnny to have a better life than he did. He doesn't want Johnny to be hurt by the world and become as hardened to it as he has.

The spirituality of *Less Than Zero* is equally unifying, but only in a surface way. All of the people around Clay are bound by a like desire to push life to the edge in a blind search for anything vaguely interesting. They depend on each other for drugs, sex, gossip, and rides home. However, this common bond isn't anything that any are willing, like Dallas and Darry in *The Outsiders,* to fight for. Their concerns center around their own problems and never seem to extend to their friends. Nowhere in the book is this better displayed than in a scene where Clay and Kim seek out an anorexic friend at Kim's New Year's Eve party and find her distraught and shooting up heroin in Kim's back bedroom. Instead of trying to save her by talking her out of it, they sit by and watch, spellbound, while she plays drug roulette.

The sacrifices that Clay and his friends are willing to make have little to do with caring about their fellow humans. As a matter of fact, they almost fall to the level of human sacrifices, as shown by their actions and lackadaisical attitude towards others. Clay finds Rip and Spin amusing themselves by having sex with a twelve-year-old girl who has sold herself to them in exchange for drugs. While Clay watches in horror and fascination, Spin shoots her up and then has sex with her. No one seems to care, including the apparently willing victim, who lies there throughout in a drug-induced stupor.

What Hinton wants to say in *The Outsiders* far transcends the realistic actions of the characters. For this reason, the novel is timeless. In the same sense, *Less Than Zero* could be symbolic of an isolated element of teenage society. The violence, gore and sex are necessary because of their direct influence upon the characters.

We are fortunate to live in a society where teenagers can be exposed to all facets of life through literature. Some would vehemently disagree, and perhaps they have valid points. Is it necessary for students to read about the almost evil, almost diabolical lifestyles of Clay and his friends? The questions that educators and parents alike need to ask are not whether it is necessary, but whether the situations exist. If they do, then teens have the right to read about them. And in so doing, maybe learn a lesson.

The Outsiders Argues That Peer Brotherhood Is the Essential Social Bond for the Disenfranchised

Lizzie Skurnick

Lizzie Skurnick has written on books and culture for the New York Times Book Review, *the* Los Angeles Times, *National Public Radio, and the* Washington Post *and maintains a noted literary blog,* Old Hag. *She is the author of* Shelf Discovery: The Teen Classics We Never Stopped Reading.

In the following article, Skurnick argues that S.E. Hinton's novels—especially The Outsiders—*demonstrate that the brotherhood offered by gangs is the primary social support network available to many boys living at the bottom rung of the socioeconomic ladder. Skurnick explains that poverty cuts lives short at youth, leaving few adults available to protect and mentor the young. This circumstance ultimately results in remarkably loyal cadres of boys relying only on each other for the nurturing and support traditionally provided by the nuclear family and its extended network.*

"S.E. Hinton is a girl?" my friend's husband, incredulous, asked me last weekend. It wasn't the first time. Given the fact that the author's *The Outsiders*, her iconic work, is still read in classrooms across the country, and that her particulars—she published the work when she was 17 as, yes, a girl—are splashed on nearly every copy, it's a perplexingly enduring question. Perhaps for readers of any age it's still difficult to believe that this profoundly diligent explorer of male adolescence, the woman who brought philosophizing, switchblade-bearing toughs with way too much hair oil and free time onto every teenager's bookshelf, probably did it in a bra.

Defying First Impressions

This misunderstanding is apropos, since one of the great themes of Hinton's *oeuvre* is the danger of reading too much into first impressions. At the outset of *The Outsiders*, the story of Ponyboy Curtis, the character introduces us to greasers, the genial hoods Hinton will follow for most of her career. As Ponyboy helpfully explains: "Greasers are almost like hoods; we steal things and drive old souped-up cars and hold up gas stations and have a gang fight once in a while. I don't mean I do things like that."

The distinction is important because when Ponyboy is implicated in the murder of a member of a rival gang, the wealthy Socs, the idea that he and his fellow greasers are more than the sum of their (slicked back) parts is crucial in making the work better than a simple us-versus-them narrative.

Brotherhood and Betrayal

But Hinton's writings go beyond even that. While *The Outsiders* is a wonderful introduction for teenagers to class strife (in one scene Ponyboy is mortified after he whips out a switchblade to dissect a frog, terrifying a genteel, pretty classmate), *West Side Story* by way of Oklahoma would get old even in the best hands. On the heels of *The Outsiders, That Was Then, This Is Now* brings in the world of the 1970s, where drugs and hippies break down the old preppies-versus-greasers, East Side/West Side dichotomy. Two friends—one drawn deeper into the neighborhood, the other trying to make a break from their petty-crime past—betray each other, one painstakingly pulling out beyond the riptide of the confusing times while

Nicolas Cage, Matt Dillon, and Chris Penn portray the brotherhood that some disfranchised youth find in gang membership in the 1983 film version of S.E. Hinton's novel Rumble Fish. © Sunset Boulevard/Corbis.

the other is crushed against the shoals. In *Tex* and *Rumble Fish*, Hinton takes the theme of brotherhood and betrayal further. While Tex spends the novel realizing his older brother is protecting, not persecuting, him by being so rough on him, in *Rumble Fish*, Rusty finds he can't be the tough legend in the neighborhood his brother was—especially once he realizes his brother wasn't either.

Parental Absence Creates a Bond

We're left to look at these distilled pairings of boys so clearly because adults are noticeably absent in this world—less out of neglect than a palpable sense that a life that cuts down so many in their youth has left few inhabitants for the upper decades. Their gaping absences—killed in a car wreck, near-dead in a hospital, on an endless leg of the rodeo circuit—leave holes in the boys' lives that they cover with pragmatic diligence, like they might tape plastic over the broken-out window of a car. What's left for the fractured families is a Lost Boys hide-out where, in a vacuum, some brothers rise to be proto-fathers and some fall into misbehaving sons, each auditioning for an adulthood they know they may not reach.

And it's in the supreme malleability of these roles that Hinton's true genius lies, as only she seems to understand that it's not the boys' rough circumstances that make them interesting but in how it's a toss-up as to whether they'll be destroyed by their world or not.

From the beginning, her hoods show amusing flashes of vulnerability, fretting about their looks (in the first paragraph, Ponyboy goes back and forth on his eye color, then finally decides, "I look better with long hair") or the looks of girls: Tex spends quite a bit of time on how he likes that his girlfriend's hair seems to have been cut in an exact bowl shape. (Perhaps hairstyles are actually Hinton's second-biggest theme: in *That Was Then, This Is Now*, Bryon can't get over how different his ex looks after his friend Mark chops off her long curls in revenge.) The older, hardened members of the greasers handle their lives in and out of jail with amusing brio, talking about getting a burger and getting in a knife fight with the same cocky irony. Hair is important, because life on the street is about substance, but it's also about style—as Ponyboy explains, using their favorite endearment for each other, which is a useful homonym:

> Tough and tuff are two different words. Tough is the same as rough; tuff means cool, sharp—like a tuff-looking Mustang or a tuff record. In our neighborhood both are compliments.

Much is made about the themes of social alienation in Hinton, but, though their world is sown with deep division, the boys of her world are not alienated at all—not from life, not from themselves, and especially not from each other. Far from an apocalyptic chaos, their code of conduct is stronger than that of heraldry. (One puts it briefly: "Our one rule is, stick together—and don't get caught.") In a world where adults are betrayers and girls are either anchors or out of reach, the primary mode is brotherhood, one in which even a cruel aside to the most vulnerable member of the gang will be slapped down by his gun-toting peers.

Hardship Stakes Their Loyalty

Scorned by the wealthy and the powerful, passing through a principal's office, the back of a police car, an ambulance, or a holding cell, Hinton's heroes don't become bitter but more loyal—to their friends, and also to the idea that they can be bigger than the social tag that's been placed on them by society. Society, uncaring, still cuts them down with great regularity. As Ponyboy tell us:

> I could picture hundreds and hundreds of boys living on the wrong sides of cities. . . . Hundreds of boys who maybe watched sunsets and looked at stars and ached for something better. I could see boys going down under street lights because they were mean and tough and hated the world, and it was too late to tell them there was still good in it, and they wouldn't believe you if you did.

But even if they're prisoner to what life hands out, they're not prisoners. Life's tough, and so are they. Why do readers go back to them again and again? Because they're also tuff.

Teachers Find *The Outsiders* Ideal for Addressing Adolescent Alienation and Class Conflict

Michael Modleski

Michael Modleski has taught in both the middle and high schools in the village of Victor, New York, for more than a decade. He largely focuses on language arts and American literature.

The following essay is drawn from Modleski's 2008 Middle School Journal *article discussing his experiences teaching* The Outsiders *to middle school students. Over the years Modleski had explored a variety of pedagogical methods to enhance the book's examination of class conflict and its impact on adolescents. He ultimately found that the key to fully leveraging the power of Hinton's novel was to deemphasize normal classroom activities (like reading-comprehension quizzes and reader-response projects), and instead focus on small-group and full-class discussions that asked the students to directly interrogate and examine the characters, their experiences, and how they react to their situations.*

At first glance, it would appear that most students in the ever growing, upscale village of Victor, New York, lead very similar lives and come from homogeneous cultural backgrounds. Of the 80 students that I see each day, not one of them is black. Two girls came from another country, but speak English relatively well. They fit right into the Victor population, and I often forget that they came from outside the United States.

Michael Modleski, "'Stay Gold,' Students: Helping Young Readers Connect to *The Outsiders*," *Middle School Journal*, vol. 40, September, 2008, pp. 12–18. Copyright © 2008 by National Middle School Association. All rights reserved. Excerpted and adapted with permission from the Association for Middle Level Education.

Unexpected Diversity

Yet, as similar as students appear, it does not take long to discover that the diversity among these students is tremendous. Neighboring the school campus is a development of homes priced in the million-dollar range. The students who wait for the bus each morning at the corner of this development have never heard mom or dad proclaim, "Sorry dear, we can't afford to eat out tonight." They come to school with their Abercrombie & Fitch uniforms, often donning makeup and perfume before stepping out to face the junior high school. Social image is the cornerstone of the adolescent lifestyle. On the other side of town, however, students awake each morning to find themselves in a vastly different situation. These students come from average or even low income families, some of which struggle daily to put food on the table for dinner. In fact, just last November, the school donated a full turkey dinner to a family that could not afford to celebrate Thanksgiving. These students sit down to eat a hurried breakfast before heading out to face the scrutiny of peers who will never understand what their life is like. This contrasting lifestyle provides the perfect forum for S.E. Hinton's novel *The Outsiders*.

Students love that *The Outsiders* was written by a 16-year-old. Each year junior high students around the country read S.E. Hinton's 50-year-old tale about life as an adolescent, and devour its universal message of acceptance and stereotype as told through the vision of a teenage author. [D.] Smith wrote, "*The Outsiders* transformed young adult fiction from a genre mostly about prom queens, football players and high school crushes to one that portrayed a darker, truer adolescent world." For 12-year-old students, the world looms overhead, stealing away their innocence one day at a time. Of course, to them, those of us who already went through adolescence have no idea what it is like. If given the opportunity to talk to S.E. Hinton, one seventh grader in Victor would tell her that, "For a teen, you wrote a sample of what happens in real life, and it's not what most adults think." In the eyes of preteens, adults memories of the cliques, the friendships created, the friendships destroyed, and the turmoil in their bodies during junior high disappeared with their graduation from high school. *The Outsiders* appeals to students because the 16-year-old author explores these issues in a way that becomes real for them.

Preparing Students to Read Hinton

I always get chills in the days before I start *The Outsiders*, when I split the classroom into two separate sides, agree and disagree. I explain to the students that I will read a series of statements to which they must respond by moving to one side of the room if they agree or the other if they disagree. I then exclaim statements such as, "Appearance can often tell a great deal about a person!" or "Anyone can be popular!" Students scramble to one side or the other, and then we debate back and forth about why they chose the side they did. Sometimes students switch halfway, and sometimes they do not, but they always come through with excruciating honesty. I love watching students learn and discuss things that they really had never considered about one another. It is a real eye-opener for everyone. I always end the activity with, "It is possible to change the way students act toward one another!" This is my favorite part of the hour, as I watch the class fight about the idealistic notion that all students can get along. One very bright, but certainly not "popular," girl shocked me this year when she explained to us that she would not want to change the way things were, because she would not want to ever be friends with the popular students. She very politely described their hurtful words, and said she was very happy not being included in their category. Several students were unable to take their eyes from the floor, and the impact was tremendous. You could have heard a pin drop as she talked. The next day, they came into class to find a copy of *The Outsiders* sitting on their desks.

We were ready to begin.

The Outsiders is so effective as a young adult novel because students immediately see the connection S.E. Hinton makes to their lives. In an article about effective reading instruction [J.] Langer contended that "[Higher performing schools] point out [real-life] connections so that students can see how the skills and knowledge they are gaining can be used productively in a range of situations." When asked if this book related to her life, one girl told me, "Yes, . . . in this book Greasers and Socs are two different cliques. They come from two different worlds." I understood that my own students came from very different worlds. There are the rich, the poor, the male, the female, the popular, and the outcasts. I knew that I would need to differentiate my teaching to reach all students. I wanted them all to feel like this book spoke to their everyday lives. I wanted it to become real. For this to occur, students needed to take control of their learning. When reading and discussing, they needed to become knowledge partners, teaching one another to acknowledge and overcome economic differences to come together as one class. During activities I sometimes grouped the class to include different types of students in each cluster, sometimes I tried to group similar students together, and once this year, I even separated the males and the females.

This year, I also decided to find out how students from the contrasting worlds received the book's message differently. I wanted to know, number one, did males and females react to the book differently, and number two, did students from different economic circles have altered interpretations of the ideas? . . .

Seeing *The Outsiders* Through Teen Eyes

A colleague of mine, whom I greatly respect and admire, often laughs when I talk about teaching *The Outsiders*. He asks mockingly, "Who names a character *Ponyboy*?" Similarly, during a discussion for a graduate class on young adult literature, I observed as the class criticized the obvious themes and moments of blatant foreshadowing that occur throughout the novel. Yet, year after year, junior high students find themselves enthralled by the characters and absorbed in the action of the story. In her groundbreaking text *In the Middle*, [N.] Atwell wrote,

> It's easy for secondary teachers to scoff at [Hinton's] novels, but she's important to adolescent readers because they identify with and love what she did in the book. Part of it is Hinton's use of fiction to explore inequities in the social situation among kids in her hometown, but most of it is her style: The narrative voice and characters are direct and compelling, and the big ideas in the novel are both evident and important to my kids.

Junior high students are not interested in the literary greatness of Faulkner and Hawthorne. However, we can rope them into literature using texts like *The Outsiders*, because the students relate to the themes and characters.

Beyond Worksheets and Quizzes

I read chapter one of *The Outsiders* aloud to wrap students up in the story. I spend the majority of the first few chapters connecting students' lives with the characters from the mid-twentieth century. We compose a T-Chart comparing Socs and Greasers and discuss Ponyboy's narrative voice. Once they understand the differences between the two groups and the rivalry that these differences cause, the class inevitably shifts toward a discussion about cliques and stereotypes. Most students immediately envision themselves as a part of one group or the other. By the end of chapter three, students no longer see *The Outsiders* as a book about gangs in the 1950s, but rather a novel about the rivalry that goes on in the hallways of their own school each and every day.

I refuse to give quizzes that test comprehension of specific details of the text. This book needs to become real to students. The quickest way to destroy that for these kids is to show them how much they failed to "understand." Atwell stated, "If [students] were to grow beyond enthusiasm and use literature as a prism for viewing and participating in the adult world, I had to figure out how to inspire them to higher, deeper purposes." To propel my students toward these higher purposes, I end chapter three posing the question, "When Johnny states, 'I can't take much more. . . . I'll kill myself or something,' what does he mean?" It forces them to use examples from the book, shows me that they read, and at the same time, it reinforces how the Greaser-Soc rivalry affects individual characters. One student responded:

> At the end of chapter three, Johnny states, "I can't take much more. . . . I'll kill myself or something." What he can't take much more of is living with this rivalry of Greasers and Socs. He can't take being jumped anymore, like the night when Steve found his jacket and then found Johnny crying. At the end of Johnny's story, Ponyboy says, "He would kill the next person who jumped him." It's showing that he can't take anymore, and that he has had enough. Also in chapter three, Johnny says, "It seems like there's gotta be somewhere without Greasers or Socs, with just people. Just ordinary people." This above all shows Johnny's hatred toward the rivalry and how he feels. Johnny is determined to get out of this. When Ponyboy says they are running away, he goes. No questions asked . . . he just wants out!

Student responses varied slightly, but the message was the same. It was time to start looking at how this rivalry affected individual characters. . . .

Fostering Lively Debate

A while back, a colleague introduced me to the concept of "The Fishbowl" discussion. Students are arranged in a circle around four desks in the center, and only the students in the center may speak. Students from the outer circle may exchange seats with those in the center when they have something to say, and all students must visit the center circle at some point during the period. For the first part of class, I hand them a sheet with topics such as these:

- After Randy and Ponyboy talk, Pony says that Randy wasn't a Soc, he was just another guy. What does he mean?

- Then at the end of the chapter, Pony notices that Cherry has green eyes. Look at the first page in the book. How is this significant?

- Do you ever label people as being a part of a group rather than an individual?

- On page 129, Cherry tells Ponyboy about Bob's ability to lead people. She says, "He had something that made people follow him, something that marked him a little different, maybe a little better than, the crowd." What if he had used that leadership differently?

- Can one person really make a difference? I tell them to create notes on the questions as if they were to be graded, then they go wild as I unleash the inner circle. They discuss cliques, friendships, the innocence of youth, the changing characters, how they can use the novel to improve the junior high, and so on. I can never predict quite where the discussion will go, and I rarely contribute. They discuss what the book means to *them*. For me, this lesson seems to drive the themes of the novel home the hardest, because, inevitably, the end of the discussion is purely based on how they can improve their own lives. Nearly 50% listed this activity as their favorite of the unit, and the enthusiasm rivals anything that I do for the remainder of the year.

Because the novel captures the students' interests so well, I often have some students that finish it in just a few days. By the time we reach the fishbowl discussion, they become impatient to reveal to others how the novel finishes, and I can see the painful looks in their eyes, as they struggle to keep the final moments to themselves. Therefore, as I allow the stragglers to read quietly in class, I allow those students who have finished the book to work in small groups, preparing to act as discussion leaders when the class confers about the final few chapters of the novel. The students who finish early are often the stronger, or at least more engaged readers, and they consistently pull through for me. They create questions such as, "Why did Dally want his friends to see him die," and, "Why do you think the doctor spoke to the judge before Ponyboy's hearing?" On discussion day, they take over, once again leaving me to smile quietly in the back of the room as these 12-year-old scholars unravel S.E. Hinton's masterpiece.

A Lasting Impact for Students

Long after we finish the novel, students discuss Johnny's character. They often list Johnny as their favorite character. Students love his self-sacrificing actions in spite of the trauma he has faced in his life. As we discuss the heroic actions of Johnny, I always ask students if they would risk their lives for others. Some adamantly believe they would, and some readily admit they would not. Either way, students admire Johnny for his courage, and his death several chapters later always brings at least one student to tears. One boy revealed that of all the parts in the book, Johnny's death affected him the most. "It made me cry a little," he admitted, only after the assurance of anonymity. Nearly 50% of his male peers agreed that this was, in fact, the part of the book that had the greatest impact. One boy even went as far as to claim that, "[Johnny's death] ruined the book!" The impact was even greater for the girls. More than 90%, all but two of the girls surveyed, listed Johnny's death as the scene with the most impact. The girls became attached to the innocence of this character, and one girl told me, "I think the end [impacted me most], when Johnny died. I felt like I knew Johnny, and when he died, it felt like losing a friend."

However, Johnny's death is not the only thing that sticks with these kids after we finish reading. Commonly, I will run into a former student in the halls and conversation will shift to *The Outsiders*. "That book was real, man," they will say, "It was the best book ever!" They so easily find a connection with the ideas presented by Hinton. Atwell stated, "Sometimes [students] see themselves as golden, fated to join the world of adults just as dawn inevitably 'goes down to day.'" Just as Johnny begs Ponyboy to "stay gold" in the moments before his death, S.E. Hinton begs these young readers not only to hold on to their youth but also to make the most of it while they can. They hear the message loud and clear.

An Education for Educators

The greatest impact for me came as I read over the surveys, recognizing the handwriting of a girl who has been given very few breaks in her life. She is well aware that her family does not have what others do, and yet always comes to school smiling and upbeat. Rather than answering the survey question by question, she wrote me this:

> I think that the most valuable lesson to be learned from the novel is that no matter what you wear or how much money you have, you're still the same to people who don't have much. I think this because people who are rich may act mean, but deep inside they are just like the rest of us. They have feelings and dreams and there is more to them than some people know; they just don't show it. I think there is something that I am going to change in my life. I think that I should make friends with people who are different from

me because for all I know they could actually be the same as me. I am also going to stop judging people by looks or how they act.

I wonder how many of her peers with all the breaks in life would agree.

Social Issues
in Literature

CHAPTER 3

Contemporary
Perspectives on
Teen Issues

Poverty and Desperation Drive Some Parents to Abandon Their Teen Children

Nordette Adams

Nordette Adams is a journalist, fiction author, and poet. She is a contributing editor at BlogHer: Life Well Said *and the African American books examiner for Examiner.com.*

In the past decade, many states have enacted "safe-haven laws," which allow parents to legally abandon infants they are unable to care for at hospitals or with emergency-response personnel. In July of 2008 Nebraska enacted one such law that, due to its wording, was interpreted by the courts to apply to all minors (that is, anyone under the age of eighteen), not just infants. During the period that this law was in effect, thirty-five children were abandoned at Nebraska hospitals over the course of four months, none of them infants. In late 2008 the Nebraska law was changed so that safe-haven provisions only applied to the abandonment of infants of up to thirty days old.

I have been turning the Nebraska child abandonment cases over in my head since I heard about them [in late September 2008]. First, two children were abandoned—a mother abandoned her 11-year-old son at one Nebraska hospital and an aunt left her 15-year-old nephew at another. Both adults indicated they couldn't handle behavior problems. Next, Gary Staton, widower and father of 10 dropped off nine of his children because he could not afford to care for them any longer and feared they'd become homeless. He said he believed the children would be better off without him.

Abandoned Children

I wouldn't want to be the parent who's come to the point where abandoning my child seems like the only option. I wouldn't want to be the abandoned child. *I don't have a solution for these families* because I don't know their full circumstances or their hearts, but I have been a depressed young mother at her wits' end, a poor parent having to ask for financial help. I've also been a child feeling that my mother doesn't love me (I was wrong), and I've been the child who's kept her parents up at night with worry. Today I'm the adult who looks back to see that my mother needed better parental coping skills, that both my parents did the best they knew how to do or could manage at one moment in time. So do I.

People, many of them angry at what they call parental irresponsibility, see the Nebraska abandonments as the inevitable result of a state law passed in July that allows parents to surrender their offspring at designated safe havens without penalty. Nebraska was the last state in the country to pass a safe haven law [as of 2008], laws written to address public concern about young mothers who've dropped their newborns in dumpsters to die and the need to protect children.

Texas, the same state in which a judge recently ordered a young woman to stop having babies, was the first state to pass a safe haven law. The Texas law allows mothers to leave infants up to 60 days in age.

Nebraska's Safe Haven Law

Nebraska lawmakers didn't want to appear backward, according to state senator Pete Pirsch (R-Omaha) in an August 18 [2008] NPR [National Public Radio] interview, and so they developed their own version of such laws with one big difference: *Under the Nebraska safe haven law, parents may abandon children as old as 19 years of age without fear of prosecution.*

In his August 18 interview, a month before the first reported case of an older child's abandonment, Pirsh, who wrote the amendment that upped the age, said the state had seen no problems at that time with parents abandoning older children. He explained to NPR that Nebraska had experienced a 2005 case in which a 2-day-old infant had been found in a canal. "The baby had been dead for two days," he told reporter Alex Cohen. And in 2007, a woman found a baby in a tote bag next to a trash bin.

He also told NPR that he advocated expansion of the bill to include older children, reasoning that if parents/caregivers are "at a point where they, out of frustration or anger, may actually injure the child then this is a vastly superior system to set up because it will take the child from that position of danger and place them in a safe environment."

Families in Financial Crisis

As a result of September's child abandonment run, Nebraska legislators are scrambling to correct what may have been a mistake. An October 2 *New York Times* [*NYT*] article examines the fallout of 14 children abandoned in one weekend, nine of which were Gary Staton's children. The article suggests that the Nebraska abandonments illuminate the stress levels for some families in financial crisis, situations perhaps worsened by our current national economic disaster, and the lack of access to adequate mental health services for even medically-insured families.

Staton surrendering nine of his 10 children has received the most attention. Over at StrollerDerby, one blogger used Staton's situation to share why she doesn't want a large family and suggests simply that Staton was irresponsible to have such a large family. The piece did not examine, and *didn't* have to, that Staton's wife died more than a year ago shortly after the birth of their 10th child, that the family had already received social service assistance, and that Staton may have been suffering, as some have suggested, from depression.

Both Staton and his wife had trouble holding down jobs, according to the *NYT* story. Giving birth so frequently seems the obvious reason behind why Staton's late wife couldn't keep a steady job, but we don't know why Staton could not stay employed or why he quit his factory job prior to "dumping" his children. . . .

Lasting Psychological Impact

[In] a blog at *The Washington Post* . . . Stacey Garfinkle asks "Does Safe Haven Law Help or Hurt?" and gives the following information:

> The National Safe Haven Alliance reports uncertainty about the exact number of children abandoned under the laws, but estimates the number at more than 2,000, according to the *New York Times*.

> In 2003, a report by the Evan B. Donaldson Adoption Institute cautioned that safe haven laws were causing more problems by encouraging women to conceal pregnancies and abandon babies rather than receive counseling and by undermining child welfare practices.

It's possible that *Baby Love Child* would agree with that assessment. She's been following the Nebraska story and believes the abandonment cases bolster her anti-safe-haven laws position. I gather that she's concerned about the emotional harm abandoned children will suffer, and stating her case, she shares the story of a 14-year-old pregnant teen abandoned in Nebraska. . . .

Baby Love Child explains her views on Nebraska's safe haven law this way:

> Nebraska legislators should be ashamed. . . . Speaking as an adoptee coming from a sealed records state, I have no way of knowing whether I was abandoned or spent time in foster care or not, but what I do know is that kids, particularly

Mother of three Lavennia Coover, who under Nebraska's safe haven law gave up her eleven-year-old mentally ill, violent son in September 2008, testifies at the Nebraska Judiciary Committee's public hearing in November 2008. © AP Images/Nati Harnik.

minors, are going to internalize this and live with the Nebraska's legislators social experimentation for the rest of their lives.

In the case of the pregnant 14-year-old, the girl's mother decided she wanted her teen back and is receiving help from her church and others.

Bringing Desperate Families to Light

One commenter on *The Washington Post* parenting blog would probably feel that a result like the one in the pregnant teen's case is exactly why safe haven laws work, and the commenter uses the willingness of Gary Staton's family to help as evidence for that belief:

> The Staton situation is being used by some people as an argument against the Safe Haven law in its present form. It is actually quite the opposite. For whatever reason, Mr. Staton was unwilling to ask for help from relatives. Yet after he left his children, some of those relatives have come forward with offers to take in the children. Mr. Staton's action was a cry for help—and the help will be provided for his children. The immediate situation is very painful for both Mr. Staton and his children. Yet we can hope that the eventual resolution will be a good one. This is precisely the intent of the Safe Haven law—to take someone's private crisis and bring it out into the open—so that, in the end, the children will be given protection. It would be a mistake to impose age limits on the law. Parents with children of any age might become overwhelmed by circumstances and not see any way out. The Safe Haven law is a clear sign to any such parents that no matter what, there is someone who will take care of their children. . . .

Keeping Kids Safe from Their Families

Blogger Bastardette is also following the Nebraska cases. She's absolutely against safe haven laws in any form or what she calls "baby dumping" laws. She interviewed National Council for Adoption President Tom Atwood, who agrees with safe haven laws for the parents of infants, but not for the parents of older children.

Atwood said, according to both Bastardette and NPR, that there is already a system in place for the parents of older children to either get help with parenting or to relinquish their parental rights by a more formal legal route. The current Nebraska line bypasses that system, he thinks.

The law was written to protect even older children who are at risk of neglect and abuse. The *NYT* article and other reports indicate officials, such as Todd A. Landry, Nebraska's state director of children and family services, do not think the recently abandoned older children were in any danger, that the parents abused the safe haven law and did not take advantage of other avenues and public resources to assist overwhelmed parents.

Nebraska State Sen. Tom White, who believes the law should allow parents to drop children at safe havens up to age 14, thinks an abandoned child is the danger signal. He said in a September 19 NPR interview that if parents are "so crazed that they will take a child to a hospital and tell them to get out, ask yourself how far are they away from hurting a child?"

Indulgent Parenting Among the Privileged Causes Teen Anxiety and Depression

Lori Gottlieb

Lori Gottlieb is a journalist, columnist, and psychotherapist. Her books include Marry Him: The Case for Settling for Mr. Good Enough.

In the following article Gottlieb explores how parents obsessed with their children's happiness and self-esteem may have inadvertently raised a generation of adults mired in indecisiveness, anxiety, and depression. She cites the views of many psychologists, teachers, and scholars who fear that when parents focus too much on catering to a child's every whim and protecting that child from every harm, they can inadvertently cause damage. Such coddled children, Gottlieb asserts, can struggle as adults with anxiety, depression, and narcissism and lack resilience and self-sufficiency.

My first several patients were what you might call textbook. As they shared their histories, I had no trouble making connections between their grievances and their upbringings. But soon I met a patient I'll call Lizzie. Imagine a bright, attractive 20-something woman with strong friendships, a close family, and a deep sense of emptiness. She had come in, she told me, because she was "just not happy." And what was so upsetting, she continued, was that she felt she had nothing to be unhappy about. She reported that she had "awesome" parents, two fabulous siblings, supportive friends, an excellent education, a cool job, good health, and a nice apartment. She had no family history of depression or anxiety. So why did she have trouble sleeping at night? Why was she so indecisive, afraid of making a mistake, unable to trust her instincts and stick to her choices? Why did she feel "less amazing" than her parents had always told her she was? Why did she feel "like there's this hole inside" her? Why did she describe herself as feeling "adrift"?

Bad Parenting Is Not to Blame

I was stumped. Where was the distracted father? The critical mother? Where were the abandoning, devaluing, or chaotic caregivers in her life?

As I tried to make sense of this, something surprising began happening: I started getting more patients like her. Sitting on my couch were other adults in their 20s or early 30s who reported that they, too, suffered from depression and anxiety, had difficulty choosing or committing to a satisfying career path, struggled with relationships, and just generally felt a sense of emptiness or lack of purpose—yet they had little to quibble with about Mom or Dad.

Instead, these patients talked about how much they "adored" their parents. Many called their parents their "best friends in the whole world," and they'd say things like "My parents are always there for me." Sometimes these same parents would even be funding their psychotherapy (not to mention their rent and car insurance), which left my patients feeling both guilty and utterly confused. After all, their biggest complaint was that they had nothing to complain about!

Too Much of a Good Thing

At first, I'll admit, I was skeptical of their reports. Childhoods generally aren't perfect—and if theirs had been, why would these people feel so lost and unsure of themselves? It went against everything I'd learned in my training.

But after working with these patients over time, I came to believe that no florid denial or distortion was going on. They truly did seem to have caring and loving parents, parents who gave them the freedom to "find themselves" and the encouragement to do anything they wanted in life. Parents who had driven carpools, and helped with homework each night, and intervened when there was a bully at school or a birthday invitation not received, and had gotten them tutors when they struggled in math, and music lessons when they expressed an interest in guitar (but let them quit when they lost that interest), and talked through their feelings when they broke the rules, instead of punishing them ("logical consequences" always stood in for punishment). In short, these were parents who had always been "attuned," as we therapists like to say, and had made sure to guide my patients through any and all trials and tribulations of childhood. As an overwhelmed parent myself, I'd sit in session and secretly wonder how these fabulous parents had done it all.

Until, one day, another question occurred to me: Was it possible these parents had done too much?

Here I was, seeing the flesh-and-blood results of the kind of parenting that my peers and I were trying to practice with our own kids, precisely so that they *wouldn't* end up on a therapist's couch one day. We were running ourselves ragged in a herculean effort to do right by our kids—yet what seemed like grown-up versions of them were sitting in our offices, saying they felt empty, confused, and anxious. Back in graduate school, the clinical focus had always been on how the *lack* of parental attunement affects the child. It never occurred to any of us to ask, what if the parents are *too* attuned? What happens to *those* kids?

Too Happy, Too Fortunate

Child-rearing has long been a touchy subject in America, perhaps because the stakes are so high and the theories so inconclusive. In her book *Raising America: Experts, Parents, and a Century of Advice About Children*, Ann Hulbert recounts how there's always been a tension among the various recommended parenting styles—the bonders versus the disciplinarians, the child-centered versus the parent-centered—with the pendulum swinging back and forth between them over the decades. Yet the underlying goal of good parenting, even during the heyday of don't-hug-your-kid-too-much advice in the 1920s ("When you are tempted to pet your child, remember that mother love is a dangerous instrument," the behavioral psychologist John Watson wrote in his famous guide to child-rearing), has long been the same: to raise children who will grow into productive, happy adults. My parents certainly wanted me to be happy, and my grandparents wanted my parents to be happy too. What seems to have changed in recent years, though, is the way we think about and define happiness, both for our children and for ourselves.

Nowadays, it's not enough to be happy—if you can be even happier. The American Dream and the pursuit of happiness have morphed from a quest for general contentment to the idea that you must be happy at all times and in every way. "I *am* happy," writes Gretchen Rubin in *The Happiness Project*, a book that topped the *New York Times* best-seller list and that has spawned something of a national movement in happiness-seeking, "but I'm not as happy as I should be."

How happy *should* she be? Rubin isn't sure. She sounds exactly like some of my patients. She has two wonderful parents; a "tall, dark, and handsome" (and wealthy) husband she loves; two healthy, "delightful" children; a strong network of friends; a beautiful neo-Georgian mansion on the Upper East Side; a law degree from Yale; and a successful career as a freelance writer. Still, Rubin writes, she feels "dissatisfied, that something [is] missing." So to counteract her "bouts of melancholy, insecurity, listlessness, and free-floating guilt," she goes on a "happiness journey," making lists and action items, buying three new magazines every Monday for a month, and obsessively organizing her closets.

At one point during her journey, Rubin admits that she still struggles, despite the charts and resolutions and yearlong effort put into being happy. "In some ways," she writes, "I'd made myself less happy." Then she adds, citing one of her so-called Secrets of Adulthood, "Happiness doesn't always make you feel happy."

Sheltering Children Can Hurt Them

Modern social science backs her up on this. "Happiness as a byproduct of living your life is a great thing," Barry Schwartz, a professor of social theory at Swarthmore College, told me. "But happiness as a goal is a recipe for disaster." It's precisely this goal, though, that many modern parents focus on obsessively—only to see it backfire. Observing this phenomenon, my colleagues and I began to wonder: Could it be that by protecting our kids from unhappiness as children, we're depriving them of happiness as adults?

Paul Bohn, a psychiatrist at UCLA who came to speak at my clinic, says the answer may be yes. Based on what he sees in his practice, Bohn believes many parents will do anything to avoid having their kids experience even mild discomfort, anxiety, or disappointment—"anything less than pleasant," as he puts it—with the result that when, as adults, they experience the normal frustrations of life, they think something must be terribly wrong.

Consider a toddler who's running in the park and trips on a rock, Bohn says. Some parents swoop in immediately, pick up the toddler, and comfort her in that moment of shock, before she even starts crying. But, Bohn explains, this actually prevents her from feeling secure—not just on the playground, but in life. If you don't let her experience that momentary confusion, give her the space to figure out what just happened (*Oh, I tripped*), and then briefly let her grapple with the frustration of having fallen and perhaps even try to pick herself up, she has no idea what discomfort feels like, and will have no framework for how to recover when she feels discomfort later in life. These toddlers become the college kids who text their parents with an SOS if the slightest thing goes wrong, instead of attempting to figure out how to deal with it themselves. If, on the other hand, the child trips on the rock, and the parents let her try to reorient for a second *before* going over to comfort her, the child learns: *That was scary for a second, but I'm okay now. If something unpleasant happens, I can get through it.* In many cases, Bohn says, the child recovers fine on her own—but parents never learn this, because they're too busy protecting their kid when she doesn't need protection.

Which made me think, of course, of my own sprints across the sand the second my toddler would fall. And of the time when he was 4 and a friend of mine died of cancer and I considered . . . not telling him! After all, he didn't even know she'd been sick (once, commenting on her head scarves, he'd asked me if she was an Orthodox Jew [Orthodox Jewish women cover their hair], and like a wuss, I said no, she just really likes scarves). I knew he might notice that we didn't see her anymore, but all of the parenting listservs I consulted said that hearing about a parent's death would be too scary for a child, and that, without lying (because God forbid that we enlightened, attuned parents ever lie to our children), I should sugarcoat it in all these ways that I knew would never withstand my preschooler's onslaught of cross-examining *whys*.

Raising Kids to Trust Themselves

In the end, I told my son the truth. He asked a lot of questions, but he did not faint from the shock. If anything, according to Bohn, my trusting him to handle the news probably made him more trusting of me, and ultimately more emotionally secure. By telling him, I was communicating that I believed he could tolerate sadness and anxiety, and that I was here to help him through it. Not telling him would have sent a very different message: that I didn't feel he could handle discomfort. And that's a message many of us send our kids in subtle ways every day.

Dan Kindlon, a child psychologist and lecturer at Harvard, warns against what he calls our "discomfort with discomfort" in his book *Too Much of a Good Thing: Raising Children of Character in an Indulgent Age.* If kids can't experience painful feelings, Kindlon told me when I called him not long ago, they won't develop "psychological immunity."

"It's like the way our body's immune system develops," he explained. "You have to be exposed to pathogens, or your body won't know how to respond to an attack. Kids also need exposure to discomfort, failure, and struggle. I know parents who call up the school to complain if their kid doesn't get to be in the school play or make the cut for the baseball team. I know of one kid who said that he didn't like another kid in the carpool, so instead of having their child learn to tolerate the other kid, they offered to drive him to school themselves. By the time they're teenagers, they have no experience with hardship. Civilization is about adapting to less-than-perfect situations, yet parents often have this instantaneous reaction to unpleasantness, which is 'I can fix this.'"

Wendy Mogel is a clinical psychologist in Los Angeles who, after the publication of her book *The Blessing of a Skinned Knee* a decade ago, became an adviser to schools all over the country. When I talked to her this spring, she said that over the past few years, college deans have reported receiving growing numbers of incoming freshmen they've dubbed "teacups" because they're so fragile that they break down anytime things don't go their way. "Well-intentioned parents have been metabolizing their anxiety for them their entire childhoods," Mogel said of these kids, "so they don't know how to deal with it when they grow up."

Which might be how people like my patient Lizzie end up in therapy. "You can have the best parenting in the world and you'll still go through periods where you're not happy," Jeff Blume, a family psychologist with a busy practice in Los Angeles, told me when I spoke to him recently. "A kid needs to feel normal anxiety to be resilient. If we want our kids to grow up and be more independent, then we should prepare our kids to leave us every day."

Selfish Parenting

But that's a big if. Blume believes that many of us today don't really want our kids to leave, because we rely on them in various ways to fill the emotional holes in our own lives. Kindlon and Mogel both told me the same thing. Yes, we devote inordinate amounts of time, energy, and resources to our children, but for whose benefit?

"We're confusing our own needs with our kids' needs and calling it good parenting," Blume said, letting out a sigh. I asked him why he sighed. (This is what happens when two therapists have a conversation.) "It's sad to watch," he explained. "I can't tell you how often I have to say to parents that they're putting too much emphasis on their kids' feelings because of their own issues. If a *therapist* is telling you to pay *less* attention to your kid's feelings, you know something has gotten way of out of whack." . . .

Wendy Mogel says that colleges have had so much trouble getting parents off campus after freshman orientation that school administrators have had to come up with strategies to boot them. At the University of Chicago, she said, they've now added a second bagpipe processional at the end of opening ceremonies—the first is to lead the students to another event, the second to usher the parents away from their kids. The University of Vermont has hired "parent bouncers," whose job is to keep hovering parents at bay. She said that many schools are appointing an unofficial "dean of parents" just to wrangle the grown-ups. Despite the spate of articles in recent years exploring why so many people in their 20s seem reluctant to grow up, the problem may be less that kids are refusing to separate and individuate than that their *parents* are resisting doing so.

"There's a difference between being loved and being constantly monitored," Dan Kindlon told me. And yet, he admitted, even he struggles. "I'm about to become an empty-nester," he said, "and sometimes I feel like I'd burn my kids' college applications just to have somebody to hang around with. We have less community nowadays—we're more isolated as adults, more people are divorced—and we genuinely like spending time with our kids. We hope they'll think of us as their best friends, which is different from parents who wanted their kids to appreciate them, but didn't need them to be their pals. But many of us text with our kids several times a day, and would miss it if it didn't happen. So instead of being peeved that they ask for help with the minutiae of their days, we encourage it."

Long work hours don't help. "If you've got 20 minutes a day to spend with your kid," Kindlon asked, "would you rather make your kid mad at you by arguing over cleaning up his room, or play a game of Boggle together? We don't set limits, because we want our kids to like us at every moment, even though it's better for them if sometimes they can't stand us." . . .

Being Too Gentle Can Hurt

Amy Chua's memoir, *Battle Hymn of the Tiger Mother*, [sparked a scathing reaction when released] earlier this year [2011]. Chua's efforts "not to raise a soft, entitled child" were widely attacked on blogs and mommy listservs as abusive, yet that didn't stop the book from spending several months on the *New York Times* best-seller list. Sure, some parents might have read it out of pure voyeurism, but more likely, Chua's book resonated so powerfully because she isn't so different from her critics. She may have been obsessed with her kids' success at the expense of their happiness—but many of today's parents who are obsessed with their kids' happiness share Chua's drive, just wrapped in a prettier package. Ours is a have-your-cake-and-eat-it-too approach, a desire for high achievement without the sacrifice and struggle that this kind of achievement often requires. When the Tiger Mom looked unsparingly at her parental contradictions, perhaps she made the rest of us squirm because we were forced to examine our own.

Chua, says Wendy Mogel, "was admitting in such a candid way what loads of people think but just don't own up to." In her practice, Mogel meets many parents who let kids off the hook for even basic, simple chores so they can spend more time on homework. Are these parents being too lenient (letting the chores slide), or too hard-core (teaching that good grades are more important than being a responsible family member)? Mogel and Dan Kindlon agree that whatever form it takes—whether the fixation is happiness or success—parental overinvestment is contributing to a burgeoning generational narcissism that's hurting our kids.

An Epidemic of Teen Violence

Jane Velez-Mitchell

Jane Velez-Mitchell is an award-winning television journalist and the author of the best-sellers Secrets Can Be Murder: What America's Most Sensational Crimes Tell Us About Ourselves; Addict Nation: An Intervention for America; *and her memoir* iWant: My Journey from Addiction and Overconsumption to a Simpler, Honest Life.

The following essay is drawn from the transcript of a 2009 episode of Velez-Mitchell's current-affairs cable program Issues with Jane Velez-Mitchell. *Over the course of their discussion, Velez-Mitchell and her panel take on what they call an "epidemic of teen violence." Among the factors they argue contribute to this epidemic are a media culture that glorifies solving problems through violence, a criminal justice system that is better at training delinquents to become criminals than at reforming wayward youths, and a lack of steadfast parenting and mentoring, especially for boys.*

Gut-wrenching teen violence rips through the country . . . a teenaged boy viciously stomped to death by a murderous mob of fellow teens in Chicago.

Now, far away in rustic New Hampshire, four teens with completely different backgrounds are accused of brutally stabbing a mother to death and hacking at her daughter with a machete.

What in the world is going on with America's teenagers? Could it have anything to do with our culture dripping in violence? . . .

An Epidemic of Teen Violence

The sick crisis of violence among our nation's kids . . . is not a city problem. It is not a race problem. It is everybody's problem. What is behind the recent twin horrors allegedly carried out by two groups of teens from totally different worlds?

First, the sadistic beating of Derrion Albert in Chicago. . . . An angry mob of teens stomped and battered the 16-year-old boy to death in broad daylight two weeks ago [September 2009]. . . .

If you're inclined to say, "Well, that's life in the inner city for you," stop yourself. Let's hop over to rural New Hampshire. . . . That's where four teenaged boys are accused of breaking into a home Sunday [October 4, 2009,] with a knife and a machete and stabbing a woman to death. . . . Police say they also critically injured her 11-year-old daughter with a machete, all so they could allegedly steal some jewelry to pawn?

Tonight's big issue: why all this teen violence? Want the answer, just look around you. Go to a movie. Flip on a video game. Channel surf, why don't you? We're a nation dripping in violence. Kids cannot avoid violent images if they tried hard. They're being indoctrinated into violent behavior.

What can we do about that? We're going to debate that right now.

Straight out to my fantastic expert panel: Tom Ruskin, former New York City police detective investigator. . . . Let's go back to Tanya Acker, and she is an attorney and blogger for *The Huffington Post*; criminal defense attorney Bradford Cohen; and clinical psychiatrist, Dr. Dale Archer.

Glorifying Violence

Dr. Dale, in the first case, it was a wild, out of control Chicago mob. In the second case, prosecutors say these four teenaged males entered the home intending to kill the occupants and allegedly proceeded to murder the mom in her bed. Officials say their goal was to rob the home with the intention of killing everyone inside.

Is there any way to explain this kind of sadism we're now seeing in the country and in the city?

DR. DALE ARCHER CLINICAL PSYCHIATRIST: Well, there's no doubt that violence has taken on epidemic status. Just a few statistics, 60 percent of kids have witnessed violence. Sixty percent of kids have been assaulted and 20 percent—20 percent—of kids have seen a shooting.

So there's no doubt it's an epidemic and there are three reasons why. And you alluded to them. One, violence on the Internet. Two, violence on TV. And three, violence in video games. Kids are seeing it every single day. And teenaged years are tough enough, always have been, but now that they have the option, kids are thinking, "You know what, they may have got the best of me but I'm going to get a gun, and I'm going to make it even."

So it is a real problem, and it's got to be addressed. And it's got to be addressed now. . . .

TANYA ACKER, ATTORNEY/BLOGGER: And I think that at the very least, Jane, we should be talking about and imagining something that approaches a civic behavior. I mean, this isn't just in video games and in television. We've completely become—started to glorify very bad behavior.

And if you look at images, if you look at role models, it is so hard these days to find somebody who exhibits the sort of behavior that people, that we would want to teach our children: behavior that shows good methods of conflict resolution, behavior that shows how to communicate effectively with people with whom you may disagree.

We don't teach that anymore. We don't glorify it. There's no role model out there like that for our kids right now, and it's very sad.

Therapy and Mentoring

VELEZ-MITCHELL: We need to talk solutions. I personally would like to see group therapy for kids starting in middle school. Again, people say, "What, are you, crazy?" No, I'm not crazy. You could use a 12-step model for group sharing that would give these children an outlet, all children, to share their emotions, to share their frustrations, to learn to talk about being angry and to talk about why they're angry without acting on the anger. That's what therapy is all about.

Rich kids have access to therapy, but poor kids in high stress, high crime urban areas who may need it the most, they don't have access to therapy.

Chicago schools have just launched a new plan. In a desperate attempt to stop the violence, school officials [are] identifying the most at-risk children. Each of them is now being assigned a mentor and offered counseling as well as a part-time job.

Tom Ruskin, you're a former New York City police detective. You've been out there on the streets.

TOM RUSKIN, FORMER NYPD DETECTIVE: Right.

VELEZ-MITCHELL: Can this work or is it Pollyanna?

RUSKIN: ... I think you're right on target with some of the ideas.

But also, schools and other people are missing the warning signs of the kids that they're dealing with. There have been many warning signs with the Columbine [High School] shooters and other people. Plus, we have to reinvent the criminal justice system to catch—catch up with these juvenile offenders.

VELEZ-MITCHELL: Yes, well, let me tell you something. Yes, Tom Ruskin, I'm going to say something a little provocative here. I think the criminal justice system is part of the problem. It's become a big business.

RUSKIN: It is part of the problem.

VELEZ-MITCHELL: We lock up more people than any other country in the world, Bradford Cohen.

BRADFORD COHEN, CRIMINAL DEFENSE ATTORNEY: It really is.

Prison Is Profitable

VELEZ-MITCHELL: And we're institutionalizing these kids and let me tell you something: somebody's making a lot of money off of it. We're warehousing them. It's totally predictable that they're going to commit a crime. And then ... We end up warehousing them and somebody makes a lot of money off of feeding them and clothing them. . . . And there's private prisons these days. We've got an industry of violence.

COHEN: Yes. And you've hit the nail on the head, because [that is] the way our system is set up. And now everyone's so scared that the kid's going to do something worse. So if you get into a schoolyard fight, they immediately send it over to the state attorney's office. The state attorney starts actions on these kids. They get sucked into the system, and it doesn't make them better. It makes them worse.

So you have a kid that may have been just a small-time nothing case and what happens is that kid starts to get worse. He gets sucked into the system. He does 21 days in a juvenile hall. He learns all these stupid things from these other kids.

VELEZ-MITCHELL: Exactly. He learns how to become a criminal.

COHEN: Correct. You come in with—with, you know, something that's very small and you leave with a lot of knowledge on a lot of crimes to commit.

VELEZ-MITCHELL: Imagine if we took all the money that we spend prosecuting, locking up, housing and warehousing these teens, who are some of them charged with first degree murder. If they kill someone, they end up spending the rest of their lives behind bars. Their families shattered.

During a trial in November 2010, New Hampshire State Police investigator Steve Puckett holds the machete a teen used in an October 2009 murder. © AP Images/Don Himsel, Pool.

But imagine if we took all that money and tried to stop them from committing that crime in the first place by addressing the underlying issues of problems in the home. The fact that they have no outlet. The fact that they have not—no knowledge of how to practice nonviolent conflict resolution. . . .

ACKER: Jane, you raised a really good point . . . about the warehousing that we're doing of kids and how they're just sort of going in and out of the system. If we could really come up with a way to capture juvenile offenders and really treat them, to do something more than just say, "Now we're going to lock you up with a whole bunch of really hardened criminals and then put you back on the street where you can demonstrate their tactics." . . .

Families in a Culture of Denial

VELEZ-MITCHELL: The problem with all of this is, if you take a look at the two cases that we're talking about today, family members of at least one suspect in both cases say, "There's no way my child could have done this." So we don't know if these children have a history of problems at this point.

A mob mentality led to death in Chicago. Four teenaged boys now charged as adults with first-degree murder. If they're convicted, they're going away forever, people. One of their moms says, "It's not my son."

Ditto with the deadly robbery in New Hampshire. Police believe the New Hampshire case, premeditated. These four young suspects all males, agreed to kill anybody who was in the secluded Mont Vernon home, say cops. This—this is the victim, a beautiful 42-year-old mom named Kimberly Cates.

Her gorgeous 11-year-old daughter, Jamie, also hacked. She barely survived. The girl bravely found the strength to call 911 and beg for help. She's now in the hospital. She could be there for a month, trying to recover.

Again, the father of the one suspect in this case—there's four suspects—but the dad of one says no way is his son a killer. . . .

About these chilling similarities. The most obvious problem, overwhelming violence in each act. Both attacks involved teenaged boys. Both involved groups of males. We're not talking about girls doing this stuff. This is testosterone. And in both cases, a relative of the suspect says, "No, it cannot be true." . . .

This is not about anti-male. This is about the fact that we have to accept, and we have to look at the fact in our country, we are equating masculinity with violence, with all these horrific movies where the man is the hunter and the woman is prey, these *Saw* type movies. We are equating masculinity with violence.

COHEN: Well, here's the problem. Jane, here's the problem with your statistics. They don't show when the—when the act of violence or the act, whatever the crime is, was sometimes motivated behind a fight over a girl or the girl pushes the guy to do something. Statistics don't show that. I'm not giving these kids any excuses. Certainly not in either of these cases. . . . I'd like to see some parenting classes, Jane. Really, if you look at both these cases, the similarities are the parents say, "Oh, this could never be my kid; it could never happen."

And if you look at a lot of violent acts, if you look at the acts that have taken place in California, you know, with the guy who ran to Canada, who allegedly murdered the young lady in California. His father, "No way [that] could be my son; no way [it] could be"—a lot of parents.

VELEZ-MITCHELL: It's called "my dog doesn't have fleas" syndrome. Yes, your dog does have fleas. . . .

Fostering Healthy Outlets for Boys

VELEZ-MITCHELL: Tanya Acker, I have to talk about what our values are as a society, because I think one of the reasons that the kids are angry is underneath [the] anger is sadness and depression. And why are they depressed? Well, I do feel that they don't have—it's a spiritual problem. They don't have the kind of outlets that they need to have a fulfilling life.

You know what graffiti is? It's a perversion of the desire to be an artist. I've done stories about kids who have been taken from doing graffiti. They're given some paint, and they become artists.

You know what rap is? It's a desire to do poetry. But yet, we look at kids today like oh, poetry, painting?

If we had—kids are pack animals. They will travel in packs when they get to be teenagers and they hit puberty. We can give them good packs, like orchestras and sports teams, or we—they will form bad packs which are called gangs.

ACKER: Absolutely right. And what we're seeing with a lot of this violence is that these kids feel powerless. And I think this is—also goes to some of the gender differences. And one of the ways that young boys in particular—not exclusively, but in particular—one of the ways in which they try to express their power is through violence.

And if we can figure out ways or really direct some of our energies toward rechanneling that, then we'd be a lot better off.

But another thing is, you know, we cannot so quickly let these parents off the hook. I mean, when we're talking about creating outlets, when we're talking about empowering kids, you know, the parents really bear bigger responsibility.

ARCHER: Right.

Returning Parents to the Equation

ACKER: I have friends who are teachers in some really, really tough school districts, and they talk about trying to get parents to come out to school meetings and . . .

ARCHER: And they won't come out.

ACKER: Absolutely. The school programs, and they are absolutely not involved. It's a real responsibility there, too.

VELEZ-MITCHELL: Well, part of that is, Dr. Dale Archer, is that a lot of the parents are young people themselves who haven't worked out their own problems and, frankly, have no business having kids, because they're not capable of being responsible parents.

ARCHER: Well, the answer is very simple in terms of the first step. Look, we have sex education classes. We have classes to just say no to drugs. We need classes about violence, because violence now is everywhere in the media.

And teenaged years have always been a very difficult time, but when you throw the option of getting a gun and shooting someone into the mix, it is time to recognize this as a bigger crisis than anything else our young people are facing today.

VELEZ-MITCHELL: And let me tell you: it's not your imagination if you think the violence is getting worse. It is.

The FBI says arrests for murders by minors has gone up 26 percent from the year 2000 to 2007. So this is a cancer on our society.

Trends in Teen Suicide

Jessica Portner

Jessica Portner is a reporter for the California newspaper the San Jose Mercury-News *and has also written for the* Christian Science Monitor *and the* Washington Post. *She has received the Education Writers Association Journalism Award and a commendation from the American Psychiatric Association for the series of articles that ultimately led to her book* One in Thirteen: The Silent Epidemic of Teen Suicide.

In the following excerpt from her book, Portner gives an overview of the current trends in teen suicide in the United States, which has seen a steep increase since the 1960s. Today one out of every thirteen teens attempts suicide, she asserts. Portner contends that suicide affects teens of both genders and all racial, ethnic, and socioeconomic backgrounds, though boys tend to use different methods than girls, opting for firearms and hanging rather than the pills preferred by girls. One method of suicide, Portner explains, is not typically recorded as such: "suicide by cop," when youths desperate to escape their lives provoke police officers to shoot them.

Which teenagers are most likely to take their own lives? Is it the popular Romeo and Juliet couple who down a lethal concoction of barbiturates and alcohol after their parents bar them from seeing each other? Or is it the quiet, academically driven student whose parents are embroiled in a messy divorce who just snaps after failing a test? Or, in the stereotype of the Columbine [High School] killers, is it the rich, narcissistic nerd who plots an elaborate and public "escape" as a revenge against the world? The answer is all of the above.

Jessica Portner, *One in Thirteen: The Silent Epidemic of Teen Suicide.* Beltsville, MD: Robins Lane Press, 2001, pp. 3–7. Copyright © 2001 by Education Week. ISBN 1-58904-001-5. All Rights Reserved. Reprinted with permission from Gryphon House, Inc., P.O. Box 10, 6848 Leon's Way, Lewisville, NC 27023. (800) 638-0928.

Universal and Frighteningly Common

No single group of children is exempt. Suicide does not discriminate by race, class, region, or gender. Upper-class urbanites, poor rural farm children, and middle-class kids crammed into minivans who become class presidents and get scholarships to Ivy League schools have all been victims of suicide.

However, in the late twentieth century, particular groups of children have contributed to the unusual surge in the nation's youth suicide rate. Self-murder among preteens and young adolescents, aged ten to fourteen, has doubled since the 1960s. Also, black teenagers in the mid-1990s were more than twice as likely to kill themselves as they were a decade earlier. But white teenagers, particularly boys, still tower over their peers in their rates of self-destructiveness.

For every teenager who commits suicide, 100 more will try. Every year, one in thirteen high school students attempts suicide, a 1997 national survey found. Half of all high school students—or about 6 million kids—say that they have "seriously considered" suicide by the time they graduate, the survey reports.

That means in a class of forty students, three will attempt suicide and twenty more will seriously contemplate it. That's an estimated 700,000 American high school students who try to end it all each year—the equivalent of every student in the Los Angeles public schools.

Differences Between Genders

Though teenagers commit suicide every day in rural communities, cities, and suburbs all across America, suicide rates have never been evenly distributed from state to state or region to region. New England has a much smaller percentage of teen suicides, while the western states, especially Montana, Colorado, Nevada, and Utah, consistently top the list. Some experts at the CDC [Centers for Disease Control and Prevention] blame the West's high rates on the relative social isolation of its residents. Some also have speculated that suicides are more common because those with a pioneering spirit who migrate west may be disappointed if they arrive at their destinations and their high expectations aren't met. If depression strikes, a psychologist may also be harder to find. Those sparsely populated states also tend to have fewer community institutions such as parks and fewer organized recreational activities to bring far-flung people together. "If people are moving all the time, those support systems may not be there and it may be harder to reach out and get help," one CDC researcher said.

Wherever they live, boys and girls tend to act very differently when it comes to planning and executing their own deaths.

While girls try to kill themselves three times as often as boys do, boys are four times more likely to finish the job. This gender gap reflects the fact that boys tend to employ more lethal means, such as firearms and hanging; girls favor more survivable methods, such as overdosing on pills. Roughly 23 percent of both male and female suicide victims hang or suffocate themselves. About 17 percent of teenage girls overdose on pills, a method chosen by only 4 percent of boys. Small percentages choose to die by drowning, in falls, or by slitting their wrists.

Male Culture and Suicides of Boys

Girls attempt suicide more than boys, experts say, because their act is an effort at communicating their desperation. Boys tend to keep their emotions hidden. "Girls cry out for help, while boys are taught to be tough and never to 'act like a girl,'" said Dr. William S. Pollack, a psychologist and professor of psychiatry at Harvard Medical School and the author of *Real Boys: Rescuing Our Sons From the Myth of Boyhood*. As a result, Dr. Pollack said, "Boys are so ashamed of their feelings, they figure they'd be better off dead" than expressing their pain.

Allison Murphy cradles the urn holding the ashes of her transgender daughter, Chloe Anne, previously named Justin Lacey, in Chloe's bedroom with Chloe's dog Ida. Chloe committed suicide in September 2010. © John Walker/ZUMA Press/Corbis.

A small percentage of the increase in teenage suicide rates could reflect improvements in reporting over the past few decades, according to Lloyd Potter, an epidemiologist and suicide expert at the CDC. But, Mr. Potter said, rates have been and continue to be artificially low because suicides are often masked or misclassified.

A child's suicide is often camouflaged by parents who rearrange the site of the death or hide suicide notes. And some medical examiners classify a death as a suicide only when a note is found, something that occurs in less than a third of all cases.

"There's no doubt there are families who don't want it to appear on the death certificate, and the coroner obliges them," said Dr. Tom Shires, a trauma surgeon with the Suicide Prevention Research Center in Nevada. In some states, Dr. Shires added, the person designated to determine the cause of death may be a lawyer or a justice of the peace with no medical training who is ill-equipped to investigate such cases.

Suicide by Cop

Dr. Shires, who is compiling a comprehensive database on suicide attempts among people of all ages, added that police are often complicit in the undercount of suicides. Law enforcement officers so consistently record single-car collisions as accidents that doctors have coined a term for them: autocides. Dr. Shires said the police file them away as accidents even when there are no skid marks on the pavement, which would indicate a desire to avoid a collision. Such misclassification throws off youth suicide rates because "unintentional injuries," primarily from automobile accidents, are the leading cause of death for fifteen- to nineteen-year-olds in the United States.

Another way suicide is hidden from the record books, say experts who study gangs, is that some teenagers who want to escape gang life but see no way out choose to die the "honorable" way by provoking police to fire at them.

"We call that 'suicide by cop,'" said Gloria Grenados, a psychiatric social worker at Bell High School in Los Angeles, a school whose students are nearly all affiliated with a gang, according to Grenados. "There are kids [who survived] who literally tell me they ran to meet the bullets because they so much wanted to die."

Taking note of such subterfuges, U.S. Surgeon General David Satcher called suicide "the nation's hidden epidemic." Suicide, Dr. Satcher said as he launched a suicide prevention campaign in the fall of 1999, must be destigmatized and addressed as a public health problem.

For Further Discussion

1. *The Outsiders* is generally applauded for its "gritty realism." Apart from Michael Malone, the authors included in this book seem to basically agree that this novel is both "gritty" and that it accurately depicts modern teen life. Do you think *The Outsiders* is realistic, or not? What details or scenes strike you as especially accurate about modern teen life? Which scenes or bits of dialogues seem unrealistic? Do your teachers and parents agree with you about which scenes are realistic and which are hokey?

2. The primary social issue in *The Outsiders* is class. S.E. Hinton strongly implies that, apart from the fact that the greasers are "low class" and the Socs wealthy, they would otherwise get along well (much as "warring" factions of greasers—like Tim Shepherd's gang and Ponyboy's—have occasional scuffles but can easily brush these off). The selections by Michael Pearlman and Eric L. Tribunella both see class as central to the novel, although they take opposing positions: Pearlman argues that *The Outsiders* ultimately helps to erase class distinctions whereas Tribunella believes the novel inadvertently reinforces them. Which do you believe is correct? Does *The Outsiders* help readers imagine ways to bridge the gap between rich and poor, or does it deepen the divide? Assuming that Hinton's novel accurately portrays class issues in 1960s Tulsa, do you observe similar class conflicts in your community? Are you surprised to learn that income inequality in the United States is greater in 2011 than it was in 1965? Why or why not?

3. Much of the mystique of *The Outsiders* is based on its popularity: Generations of young adult readers have read

the book eagerly, passed it to friends, numbered it among the "best things" they ever read in school, and grew to pass it on to their own children. Most of the selections in this book have at least passingly mentioned the novel's ongoing popularity. A few have also asserted that the book's writing is somewhat weak. Only Michael Malone really takes fans to task for applauding what he views as, apart from its popularity, a rather mediocre—and occasionally laughable—debut novel. While teachers and librarians will acknowledge that Hinton's writing and plotting can be clumsy, they nonetheless continue to recommend the book, both because it appeals to young readers and because it addresses social issues—especially the impact of class and poverty on teens—that otherwise go ignored. Is it more important for schools to promote excellently written literature, or to select books that are useful for classroom discussions? If you were a teacher, would you use *The Outsiders* in class? Why or why not? Do you think Ponyboy would agree with your reasoning? What about Johnny? Explain.

4. *The Outsiders* is an especially well-loved book among teachers and school librarians because many students (especially those otherwise uninterested in reading) connect with this novel. According to Michael Modleski, this visceral connection allows his students to engage in much deeper critical analysis of the text than is possible with other—arguably more relevant or valuable—literature. Did you personally connect with *The Outsiders* in the way Modleski and many other authors contributing to this volume have described? Why or why not? Even if many students did not connect with the novel, can you explain why teachers might still want to use it in class? What are the factors teachers should take into account when they select classroom materials?

For Further Reading

Laurie Halse Anderson, *Speak*. New York: Farrar, Straus & Giroux, 1999.

Anonymous, *Go Ask Alice*. New York: Simon & Schuster, 1971.

Judy Blume, *Forever . . . : A Novel*. Scarsdale, NY: Bradbury Press, 1975.

Robert Cormier, *The Chocolate War*. New York: Pantheon Books, 1974.

S.E. Hinton, *Rumble Fish*. New York: Delacorte, 1975.

S.E. Hinton, *Some of Tim's Stories*. Norman: University of Oklahoma Press, 2007.

S.E. Hinton, *Taming the Star Runner*. New York: Delacorte, 1988.

S.E. Hinton, *Tex*. New York: Delacorte, 1979.

S.E. Hinton, *That Was Then, This Is Now*. New York: Viking, 1971.

Walter Dean Myers, *Monster*. New York: HarperCollins, 1999.

Walter Dean Myers, *Motown and Didi: A Love Story*. New York: Viking, 1984.

W.R. Philbrick, *Freak the Mighty*. New York: Blue Sky Press, 1993.

Adam Rapp, *33 Snowfish*. Cambridge, MA: Candlewick Press, 2003.

Cynthia Voigt, *Homecoming*. New York: Atheneum, 1981.

Paul Zindel, *The Pigman*. New York: Harper & Row, 1968.

Bibliography

Books

Dennis Abrams	*S.E. Hinton.* New York: Chelsea House, 2009.
Allan Creighton and Paul Kivel	*Helping Teens Stop Violence, Build Community, and Stand for Justice.* Alameda, CA: Hunter House, 2011.
Jimmy Dorrell	*Plunge2Poverty: An Intensive Poverty Simulation Experience.* Birmingham, AL: New Hope, 2007.
Fran Fearnley and Fred Matthews	*I Wrote on All Four Walls: Teens Speak Out on Violence.* Toronto: Annick Press, 2004.
Irving B. Harris	*Children in Jeopardy: Can We Break the Cycle of Poverty?* New Haven, CT: Yale University Press, 1996.
Marylou Morano Kjelle	*S.E. Hinton: Author of "The Outsiders."* Berkeley Heights, NJ: Enslow, 2007.
Ruby K. Payne and Paul D. Slocumb	*Boys in Poverty: A Framework for Understanding Dropouts.* Bloomington, IN: Solution Tree, 2010.
Karen Sternheimer	*Kids These Days: Facts and Fictions About Today's Youth.* Lanham, MD: Rowman & Littlefield, 2006.

Eric L. Tribunella   *Melancholia and Maturation: The Use
of Trauma in American Children's
Literature.* Knoxville: University of
Tennessee Press, 2009.

John M. Violanti   *Copicide: Concepts, Cases, and
and James J.   Controversies of Suicide by Cop.*
Drylie   Springfield, IL: Charles C. Thomas,
2008.

Antoine Wilson   *S.E. Hinton.* New York: Rosen, 2003.

Youth   *Things Get Hectic: Teens Write About
Communication   the Violence That Surrounds Them.*
New York: Touchstone, 1998.

Periodicals

Christopher   "The Power of Male Relationships,"
Bantick   *Asia Africa Intelligence Wire,*
November 2004.

Susannah Bowyer   "A History of Neglect Around
Adolescent Mistreatment,"
Community Care, March 24, 2011.

Vincent Canby   "*Outsiders,* Teen-Age Violence," *New
York Times,* March 25, 1983.

Paul J. Fink   "Exposure to Violent Media Results
in Brain Changes That Might
Desensitize Teen Boys to Aggression.
Should We Advise Patients in
Therapy to Stay Away from Violent
Media?" *Clinical Psychiatry News,*
December 2010.

Jeffrey Kaplan — "Perception and Reality: Examining the Representations of Adolescents in Young Adult Fiction," *ALAN Review*, Fall 2008.

Yvonne Litchfield — "Her Book to Be Published Soon, but Tulsa Teen-Ager Keeps Cool," *Tulsa Daily World*, April 7, 1967.

Denise Rinaldo — "Poor in a Land of Plenty: Meet Three Teens Who Are Vowing Not to Let Poverty Hold Them Back," *Scholastic Choices*, April–May 2005.

Ron Schachter — "Pursuing Peace in Chicago: Ron Huberman Has Spent His First Year as School's CEO Confronting an Epidemic of Urban Teen Violence," *District Administration*, February 2010.

Seventeen — "Face to Face with a Teen-Age Novelist," October 1967.

Dave Smith — "Hinton, What Boys Are Made Of," *Los Angeles Times*, July 15, 1982.

Barbara White Stack — "Juvenile Court Journal: Teens Often Left Behind," *Pittsburgh Post Gazette*, February 10, 2002.

Steven L. VanderStaay — "Doing Theory: Words About Words About *The Outsiders*," *English Journal*, November 1992.

Jane Velez-Mitchell — "Florida Teen Set on Fire by Other Teens" (Broadcast transcript), *Issues with Jane Velez-Mitchell*, October 13, 2009.

Internet Sources

Associated Press   "Nebraska Law Allows Abandonment of Teens: 'Safe-Havens' Potentially Permit Parents to Drop Off Kids as Old as Nineteen," August 22, 2008. www.ap.org.

Danah Boyd   "Viewing American Class Divisions Through Facebook and MySpace," *Apophenia Blog Essay*, June 24, 2007. www.danah.org.

Hillel Italie   "S.E. Hinton Reflects on *The Outsiders*," Associated Press, September 29, 2007. www.ap.org.

Scott Michels   "Nebraska Safe Haven Law Draws Criticism," ABC News, October 9, 2008. http://abcnews.go.com.

Index